THE UTAH STORY

SETH SORENSEN

THE
UTAH
STORY

SETH SORENSEN

BONNEVILLE BOOKS
SPRINGVILLE, UTAH

Mammoth picture on page 9 appears courtesy College of Eastern Utah.

ISBN: 978-1-59955-473-0

Published by Bonneville Books, an imprint of Cedar Fort, Inc., 2373 W. 700 S., Springville, UT 84663
Distributed by Cedar Fort, Inc., www.cedarfort.com

LIBRARY OF CONGRESS CATALOGING-IN-PUBLICATION DATA

Sorensen, Seth Val, 1975-
  The Utah story / Seth Val Sorensen.
    p. cm.
  Summary: A short history of the state of Utah.
  ISBN 978-1-59955-473-0
  1. Utah--History. I. Title.
  F826.S67 2010
  979.2--dc22

                      2010029359

Cover design and page layout by Angela D. Olsen
Cover design © 2011 by Lyle Mortimer
Edited by Heidi Doxey

Printed in China
10 9 8 7 6 5 4 3 2
Printed on acid-free paper

CONTENTS

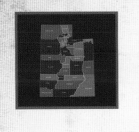

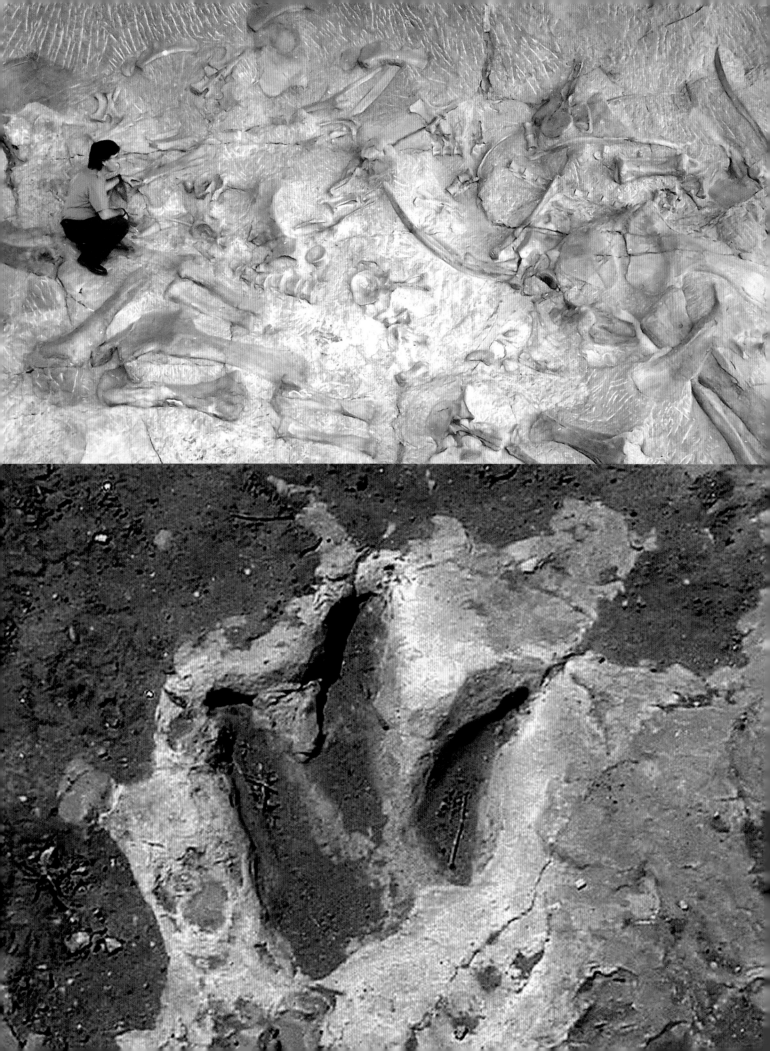

THE
BEGINNING

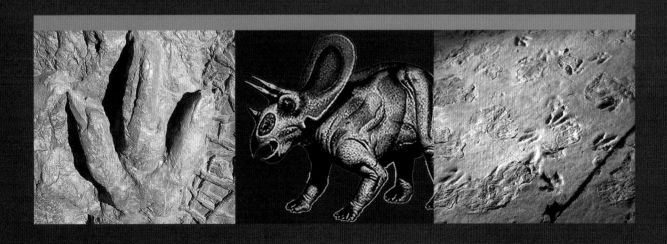

PANGAEA

Our Utah's story begins millions of years ago, long before humans even existed. This is a time when all of the land in the world was joined together in a giant continent called **Pangaea.** This was a time when great seas covered much of the western United States. It was a time when the world looked much different and Utah was not much more than an inland sea.

During this time, dinosaurs did not yet walk the land; creatures such as **trilobites, ammonites, snails,** and a variety of other aquatic animals ruled Utah. Their remains can still be found throughout the state, providing proof of their lives and existence. To this day you can still find their fossils in the Wasatch and Manti LaSal Mountains, as well as in Utah's West Desert near Delta.

THE MESOZOIC ERA

Let's jump ahead to a time when the continents were breaking up and resembled more closely their current shapes. This was a time when giants roamed Utah and the inland sea had pulled back. It was the time of the dinosaurs.

Dinosaurs only lived during a period of time known as the **"Mesozoic Era,"** which is often called the "Age of Dinosaurs." Utah has some of the best Mesozoic rock record in the entire world; because of this, we have a tremendous fossil record from the time of the dinosaurs.

The Mesozoic Era, which went from 225 to 65 million years ago, is divided into three time periods: the **Triassic** (225–193 million years ago), the **Jurassic** (193–136 million years ago), and the **Cretaceous** (136–65 million years ago). The first dinosaurs did not exist in the world until the end of the Triassic period, and they did not exist in Utah until the Jurassic period.

TRILOBITE

THE JURASSIC PERIOD

During the early and middle part of the Jurassic period, Utah was for the most part a desert, although from time to time the sea level would rise and cover the desert. Dinosaur footprints have been found in many places in Utah dating from this time, but no dinosaur skeletons have yet been found in the rocks from this period.

Nearly all of Utah's best-known dinosaur fossils are from dinosaurs that lived during the late Jurassic period. They are found in a rock formation known as the **Morrison Formation,** which dates back about 150 million years.

Utah in the late Jurassic period would have been a terrifying place. Incredible monsters roamed the land. King among these was **Allosaurus.** At the Cleveland Lloyd Quarry, Allosaurus is by far the most numerous fossil, and at least 44 individuals have been found. These ranged in size from juveniles of about 3 feet in length to adults of about 39 feet. Some weighed nearly as much as an elephant.

ALLOSAURUS FACTS

NAME: Allosaurus

PRONUNCIATION: all-oh-SA-rus

MEANING: Different Lizard—It had strange looking vertebrae

ANIMAL TYPE: Dinosaur (Therapod)

DIET: Carnivore—It hunted other dinosaurs

SIZE: Up to 40 feet long

WEIGHT: Up to 3 tons

MAJOR FOSSIL FINDS: Utah, Wyoming, New Mexico, Tanzania

Allosaurus is Utah's **STATE FOSSIL**

ALLOSAURUS

ALLOSAURUS
SKELETON

ALLOSAURUS

Utah's State Fossil is the Allosaurus. Allosaurus was a large, meat-eating dinosaur; in fact, it was the biggest meat-eater in North America during the late Jurassic period. Allosaurus was a powerful predator that walked on two muscled legs, had a strong, S-shaped neck, and had vertebrae that were different from those of other dinosaurs (Allosaurus means "different lizard"). It had a massive tail, a bulky body, and heavy bones. Its arms were very short, and it had three-fingered hands with sharp claws that were up to 6 inches (15 cm) long.

Allosaurus reached up to 39 feet long (12 m) and 17 feet tall (5 m). It weighed about 6,000 pounds. It had a 3-foot-long (90 cm) skull with two short brow-horns above its eyes, and bony knobs on the top of the head. It had large jaws with sharp, serrated teeth that could be 2 to 4 inches (5 to 10 cm) long.

Allosaurus's legs were about 4 feet long. Its stride length (the distance when it stepped) was almost 8 feet. Allosaurus's femur (thigh bone) was about 30 inches (77 cm) long. That is nearly 3 feet.

Scientists have wondered whether or not the large, short-armed dinosaurs that walked on two legs (like T. Rex, Albertosaurus, and Allosaurus) would run very fast because if they fell, their arms would be too short to break their fall and they would be badly injured. This meant that these large hunters would be slow, lumbering animals.

New discoveries by scientists indicate many of these animals had suffered broken ribs that had healed. It is thought that these were caused by falls as the animals were running at great speeds. Some fossils even show ribs that have been broken, healed, and then broken again—and the dinosaurs survived. This helps confirm the fact that these creatures were hunters that chased down their prey.

The Utah state legislature made Allosaurus the state dinosaur in 1988. More Allosaurus fossils have been found in Utah than any other dinosaur. To date, over sixty have been discovered.

Also found among the fossils in Utah rock is the **Apatosaurus,** better known as **Brontosaurus.** Apatosaurus grew up to 90 feet long and could weigh more than 30 tons, or as much as six elephants.

Another giant of this era was **Brachiosaurus,** which is among the largest animals that ever lived on planet Earth. Brachiosaurus weighed nearly 80 tons, or as much as 15 grown elephants.

Diplodocus was another giant of this time period. A relative of the Apatosaurus, Diplodocus reached lengths of over 87 feet. Several nearly complete skeletons of this ancient animal have been found at Dinosaur National Monument.

Stegosaurus, the plated dinosaur, is one of the better-known Utah plant-eaters of the Jurassic period. Paleontologists believe Stegosaurus's distinctive triangular bony

BRACHIOSAURUS

STEGOSAURUS

ACROCANTHOSAURUS

UTAHRAPTOR

plates were staggered in a set of two rows along its back. The reason for these plates is unknown, but perhaps they were for protection or to gather solar radiation to keep their bodies warm. Even though Stegosaurus is the state dinosaur of Colorado, it is very common in Utah.

THE CRETACEOUS PERIOD

Utah's early Cretaceous period would have been just as frightening. **Acrocanthosaurus** would have been the supreme dinosaur of this period. It was as large as Tyrannosaurus, having a 4.5-foot-long skull and 68 thin, sharp, serrated teeth. Acrocanthosaurus was a fierce predator that was roughly 30–40 feet long and weighed about 5,000 pounds. Acrocanthosaurus (meaning "high-spine lizard") had 17-inch spikes extending from its vertebrae, along the neck, back, and tail, that may have formed a thick, fleshy sail on its back. It had powerful arms, and each hand had three fingers, equipped with long, sickle-like claws.

The **Utahraptor** was another terrifying carnivore that lived during this time. The Utahraptor was the giant version of the famous Velociraptor. It had four-toed feet; the second toe had a 9–15-inch sickle-like claw, and the other toes had smaller claws. Its long tail had bony rods running along the spine, giving it rigidity; the tail was used for balance and fast turning ability. It had a relatively large brain and large, keen eyes. Utahraptor was 16–23 feet long and may have weighed about 1 ton.

Another famous dinosaur of this early Cretaceous period was **Iguanodon**. Iguanodon was a dinosaur that had a toothless beak and tightly packed cheek teeth. On each hand, Iguanodon had four fingers and a short thumb spike. The thumb spikes may have been used for defense or to obtain food and ranged from 2 to 6 inches long. Iguanodon had a flat, stiff tail and three-toed hind feet with hoof-like claws. Iguanodon averaged about 30 feet long and 16 feet tall and may have weighed 4 to 5 tons.

The late Cretaceous period saw what is probably the most famous of all dinosaurs roaming the lands of Utah, **Tyrannosaurus Rex.** It had serrated teeth that were as large as a banana. These teeth were used to crush the flesh and bone of its prey. With a massive head and jaws that measured more than 5 feet in length, a body length of up to 50 feet, and a weight of up to 7 tons, an adult Tyrannosaurus was the largest of the predatory dinosaurs. It was also the last, living only at the very end of the Cretaceous period, 65 million years ago.

Another giant that occupied this period was

the **Torosaurus.** This giant three-horned animal is often mistaken for a Triceratops because of the three horns and large bone frill on its head. Torosaurus was as large as an elephant, and its enormous frill was modified from the bones in the rear part of its head, giving it a skull over 10 feet

TYRANNOSAURUS REX

TYRANNOSAURUS REX
SKELETON

TOROSAURUS

long (the largest of any land animal). Its three horns served to protect the front of its body, making even Tyrannosaurus think twice about attacking a full-grown adult.

Parasaurolophus was another large herbivore best known for the large trombone-shaped crest on its head. This hollow crest is thought to have been used as a resonating chamber for making sounds used to communicate with others of its kind. The crest may also have been used for display or for giving it an improved sense of smell.

TRICERATOPS SKULL

OUCH!

Some dinosaurs swallowed large rocks, called gastroliths, to help grind and digest their food. These rocks sometimes weighed up to 10 to 20 pounds.

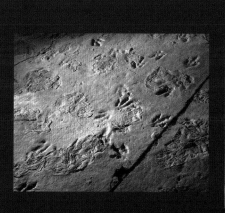

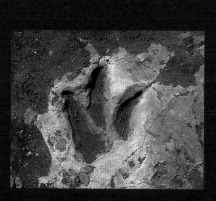

UTAH'S HIDDEN HISTORY

Dinosaur tracks can still be found throughout Utah. During the time of dinosaurs, Utah mud and clay was perfect for leaving footprints wherever dinosaurs walked. As the mud and clay dried, the tracks often filled in with more sand and dirt. The mud and clay eventually turned to stone over millions of years, leaving the dinosaur footprints for us to see today. One of the best places to see a lot of dinosaur footprints in one location is Johnson's Farm near St. George.

THE
ICE AGE

THE ICE AGE

LAKE BONNEVILLE

Now we move ahead to Utah's "Ice Age." As the inland seas retreated, a massive lake was formed, **Lake Bonneville.** At its largest, Lake Bonneville was nearly 325 miles long, 135 miles wide, and was up to 1,000 feet deep in places. Many of the islands that would have existed in the lake are the present-day mountain ranges of western Utah. Its relatively fresh water came from rain, snow, rivers, streams, and melting glaciers.

Many types of fish, including Utah's state fish, the **Bonneville Cutthroat,** inhabited the lake. A large variety of animals patrolled the

BONNEVILLE CUTTHROAT

Hear ye! Hear ye! Because of Senate Bill 236 in 1997, the Bonneville Cutthroat replaced the rainbow trout as Utah's state fish after having the rainbow trout since 1971. The Bonneville Cutthroat has been native to Utah since before the time of Lake Bonneville and was important to the Utah natives and Mormon pioneers as a source of food.

BONNEVILLE CUTTHROAT

Modern Day
The Great Salt Lake

Lake Bonneville

WAVE-CUT PLATFORMS FROM
LAKE BONNEVILLE

edge of the lake, including many animals that still exist in Utah today such as **deer, bighorn sheep, bison,** and **pronghorn antelope.**

There were also animals that you would not have expected to find here, such as **camels** and **horses,** which became extinct at the end of the ice age. The ice age was also a time when strange animals roamed Utah in large numbers. The giant **mammoths** and **mastodons,** ancient but distant relatives of modern elephants, were both found throughout the state. If you were to visit then, you would also have found **musk oxen,** which now only live in the far north of the American continent, **giant ground sloths,** and even **saber-toothed cats** and **short-faced bears.**

UTAH'S ICE AGE ANIMALS

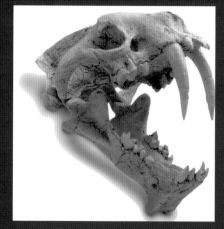
SABER-TOOTHED CAT

BIGHORN SHEEP

PRONGHORN ANTELOPE

CAMEL

MUSK OX

AMERICAN BISON

GIANT GROUND SLOTH

UTAH'S HIDDEN HISTORY

The short-faced bear was the largest, and probably the most powerful, of Utah's Ice Age predators. On all fours, this bear stood 5 feet tall at the shoulders, making it larger than the modern grizzly, brown bear, and polar bear of North America. When standing upright, a large short-faced bear was up to 12 feet tall and could weigh as much as 1,800 pounds. Its teeth suggest that this bear, like modern grizzlies and black bears, was an omnivore, meaning it ate both plants and animals.

SHORT-FACED BEAR

SHORT-FACED BEAR

POLAR BEAR

GRIZZLY BEAR

BEAR SIZE COMPARISON

MAMMOTH FOUND IN CENTRAL UTAH

On August 8, 1988, a bulldozer operator working on the Huntington Reservoir Dam in central Utah found the Huntington Mammoth when he uncovered a front leg bone and a section of the tusk. The skeleton of the mammoth was 27 feet long and was about 90 percent complete. The mammoth lived about 10,500 years ago, very close to the time when mammoths went extinct. Mammoths, like elephants, live to be very old. This mammoth was a very old individual, as indicated by worn teeth and arthritis in its bones. Casts of the Huntington Mammoth's skeleton can be seen at the Fairview Museum in Fairview, the Utah Museum of Natural History in Salt Lake City, and the College of Eastern Utah (CEU) Prehistoric Museum in Price. The jawbone of a giant short-faced bear was also found at the site. The bear is thought to be 400 years younger than the mammoth. It is believed that the bear had been feeding on the frozen remains of the mammoth when it too passed away.

EXTRA! EXTRA!

August 8, 1988

MAMMOTH
Found in Central Utah

THE FIRST HUMANS

Scientists believe that humans arrived on the Utah Ice Age scene about 10,000 years ago. These early Utahns were **hunters and gatherers,** meaning they hunted for their food and gathered plants and berries. They used primitive stone tools to hunt for animals such as mammoths, deer, and other ice-age creatures. Many of these tools have been found throughout the state.

It did not take long for these **nomads** to claim sections of the state and use these as their territories. These groups eventually became the Native American Tribes of Utah. Some of the earliest recognized in Utah were the Fremont and the **Anasazi** (Ancestral Puebloan). These two groups built much more permanent homes, which can still be seen today. Fremont Indian State Park and Anasazi State Park are some of the best preserved of these groups' dwellings.

FREMONT INDIANS

The Fremont Indians received their name from the Fremont River in Utah where the first Fremont sites were discovered. Fremont Indian State Park in south-central Utah is the largest Fremont site in Utah. A more recent discovery of a new site at Range Creek has also caused a great deal of interest because it managed to stay undisturbed for centuries. Nearby Nine Mile Canyon has long been

FREMONT PETROGLYPHS

known for its large collection of Fremont rock art, dating back over a thousand years. Other sites are found in Dinosaur National Monument, Zion National Park, and Arches National Park.

The Fremont lived a lifestyle that revolved around hunting deer and rabbits, gathering edible plants, and growing corn for food. They lived in pit houses and made everything from dishes to dolls from the clay they gathered from the soil.

ANASAZI INDIANS

The Anasazi (Ancestral Puebloan) Indians lived in homes built into the sides of cliffs called **cliff dwellings.** These dwellings were made from a combination of stone, clay, and mud placed together much like modern day bricks. Many of these cliff dwellings can still be seen in southeastern Utah.

FREMONT INDIAN CLAY DOLLS
(Photo use courtesy of CEU Prehistoric Museum in Price)

ANASAZI DWELLINGS AT DARK CANYON

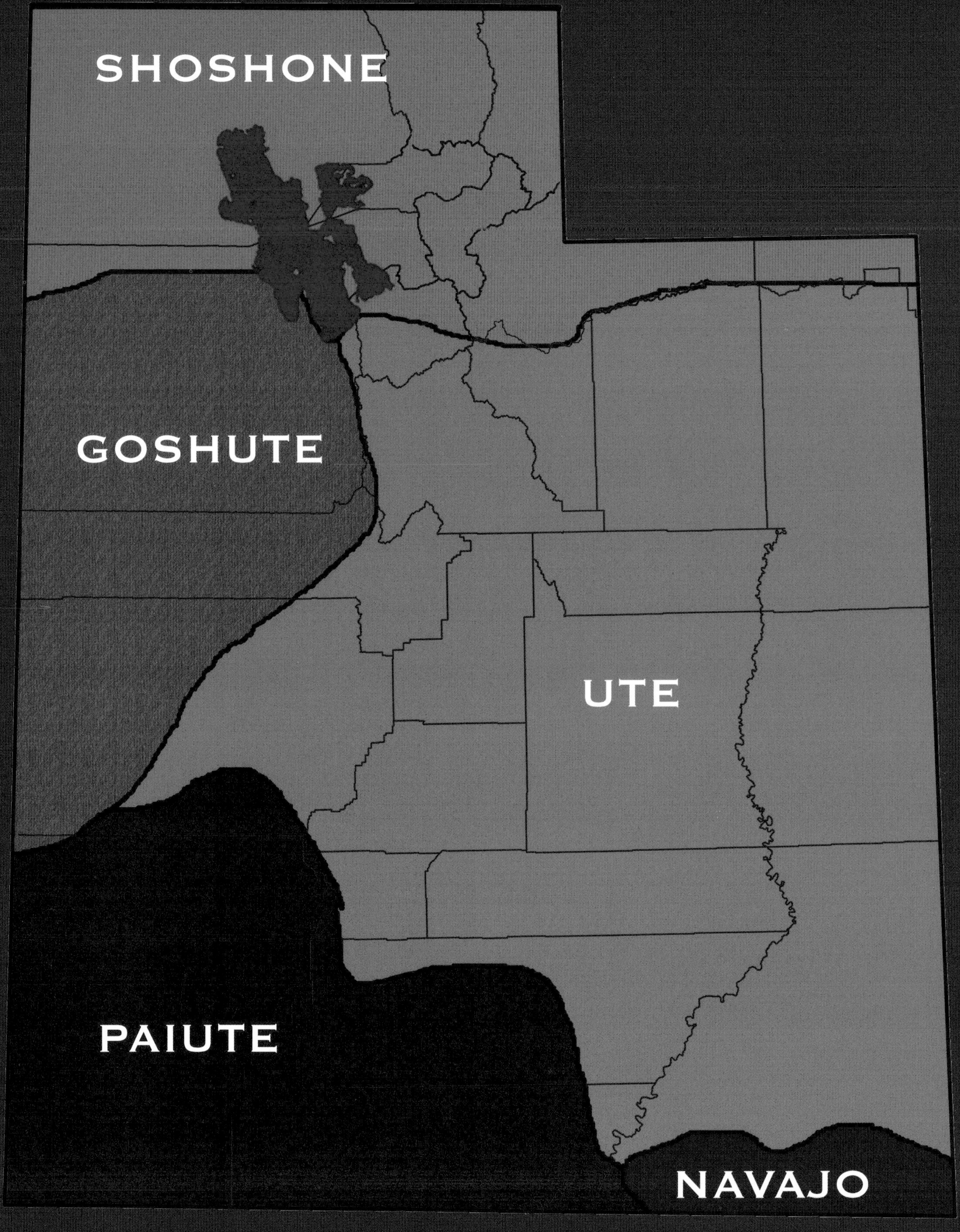
SHOSHONE
GOSHUTE
UTE
PAIUTE
NAVAJO

FIVE
NATIVE
TRIBES

Five Native Tribes

As we jump forward in time a bit, we now take a look at Utah's five major native tribes. These tribes are the **Ute, Navajo (Dine'), Paiute, Goshute,** and **Shoshone.** These tribes make up much of Utah's history before the arrival of the first European settlers in the 1800s.

Ute

The state of Utah was named after the **Ute** Tribe, which means, "Land of the Sun." Before the arrival of settlers, part of this group occupied the Provo Valley area of what is now Utah County. The Ute's religious beliefs were based in nature, with animals serving as the central deities, or gods. The Ute believed they were closely related to the bear, an animal that is common in their myths and stories. The Ute shaman, or religious leader, was believed to be very powerful, and it was thought he could communicate with nature and the gods. In the spring, the Ute would gather for the annual Bear Dance, also known as "Moma-qui Mowat," followed in the summer by the Sun Dance, which were their most important social and religious ceremonies.

The Ute were not originally farmers and did not traditionally grow crops. The Ute way of life was greatly influenced by Europeans such as the Spanish, who introduced them to horses, which the Ute referred to as "Magic Dogs," and of course, the Mormon settlers, who introduced them to farming. Soon, the Ute were raising livestock, utilizing the land, and, thanks to the added convenience of being able to ride on horseback, hunting buffalo, which were practically wiped out of existence in Ute land. Eventually, the Ute became great traders of both livestock and slaves, who were their conquered enemies whom they sold into labor.

Navajo

The **Dine',** or **Navajo,** religious beliefs were based on keeping health and harmony in a person's life. The **Hatalii,** or medicine man, was a key person in every aspect of their lives. The Hatalii went through years of training and work to be qualified for the position, just as we do with our schooling today. This training included memorizing the sacred chants, learning about herbs and plants, and even learning to identify what type of sickness

UTE CHIEF OURAY AND HIS WIFE, CHIPETA

NAVAJO HATALII

NAVAJO HOGANS

PAIUTE INDIANS

a troublemaker and joker who enjoyed causing trouble.

The Paiute's lifestyle was adapted to the harsh desert environment in which they lived. Each tribe or band occupied its own specific area or territory. Rabbits, mountain sheep, waterfowl, and deer were often hunted in surrounding areas. Pinion nuts, gathered in the mountains during the fall, provided important food for the winter. Grass seeds and roots were also an important part of their diet.

Unlike some tribes, Paiute chiefs had very limited power, and their authority was based on their ability to work well with others. In most cases, leadership among the Paiute was based on the skill or ability to perform a task. If you were the best at hunting deer, you were in charge of hunting deer; if you were best at making baskets, you would be in charge of making baskets.

a member of their tribe might have. In many ways they were much like modern doctors in their responsibilities to the community.

The Navajo were farmers and hunters. They grew corn and other plants for food and hunted bison, deer, and rabbits. The Navajo also grew other plants for the purpose of weaving beautiful clothing, blankets, and rugs. They also made beautiful pottery and dishes from clay.

GOSHUTE

The **Goshute** lived in the area between the Great Salt Lake and Utah Lake. The Goshutes hunted and gathered in small family groups. Because they lived in the harsh desert, they paid close attention to the seasons and how the plants and animals changed with the seasons.

MONUMENT VALLEY

PAIUTE

The **Paiute** were located in the southwest part of Utah, in what is now Washington County. The religious world of the Paiutes revolved around the wolf and coyote. Wolf was the elder brother and the more responsible god, while Coyote was

COYOTE

Because of their location, the Goshute were the last to be affected by settlers moving west. As their lands were settled and used for grazing by livestock, the traditional plants and animals the Goshute used for food disappeared. The settlers even used up their family water sources for their animals. As all of this happened, the Goshutes responded in the only way they could—by attacking the settlers.

THE BLACK HAWK WAR

The Black Hawk Indian War was the longest and most destructive conflict between pioneer immigrants and natives in Utah's history. The war officially began on April 9, 1865, but tensions had been mounting for years. On that date a group of Utes and Mormon frontiersmen met in Manti, Sanpete County, to settle an argument over some cattle that were killed and eaten by the starving tribe. An irritated settler lost his temper and violently jerked a young chieftain from his horse. This insulted the natives, including a young Ute named Black Hawk, who quickly left, promising retaliation. Over the next few days, Black Hawk and other Utes killed five Mormons and escaped to the mountains with hundreds of stolen cattle. Naturally, many hungry Ute men and their families came to eat the stolen beef and to support Black Hawk, who was now hailed as a war chief.

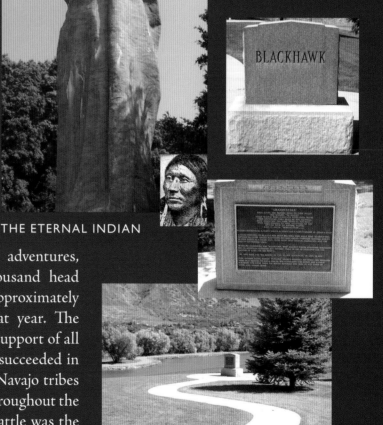

THE ETERNAL INDIAN

Black Hawk continued his adventures, stealing more than two thousand head of livestock and killing approximately twenty-five more settlers that year. The young chief did not have the support of all of the tribes of Utah, but he succeeded in uniting the Ute, Paiute, and Navajo tribes into an army, which moved throughout the Mormon territory. Stealing cattle was the main thing that Black Hawk's warriors did, but travelers, herdsmen, and settlers were also killed at times. Some estimates show that as many as seventy settlers were killed during the Black Hawk War.

In the fall of 1867, Chief Black Hawk made peace with the Mormons. Without his leadership, the native forces found it difficult to work together and organize raids. The fighting decreased, and a peace treaty was signed in 1868. Some raiding and killing continued until 1872, when 200 federal troops were finally ordered to step in and end the conflict. Chief Black Hawk died of tuberculosis on September 26, 1870.

BLACKHAWK

CHIEF BLACK HAWK'S GRAVE

Over time, treaties were signed, and the Goshute took up farming and ranching as a means of obtaining food.

SHOSHONE

The **Shoshone** lived in small family groups. They believed in the strong spiritual powers of both plants and animals and treated them with great respect. In many cases, their shaman would visit the herds of pronghorn antelope, sing to the animals, sleep with them, and help drive them to a brush corral, where they could be shot. The pinion nut harvest was also a time of important religious ceremonies, and the people regarded the pinion-gathering areas as very sacred.

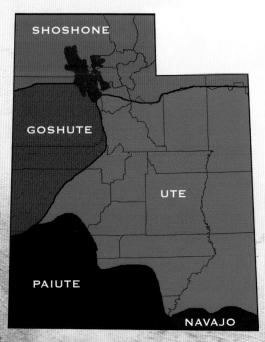

SHOSHONE TEEPEES

The Shoshone were hunters and gatherers. Animals used by the Shoshone included beaver, elk, porcupines, bobcats, rabbits, otters, badgers, bears, and sometimes even mountain lions.

The hunters were often careful not to kill the female animals, birds, and fish during times when they would be having babies or caring for their young. The Shoshone also ate such plants as thistles, sagebrush seeds, the leaves and roots of arrowleaf, buffalo berries, pine nuts, sego lilies, wild rye seeds, Indian ricegrass, and cattails.

AXE, AWL, AND ARROWHEAD

TRADITIONAL UTAH TRIBAL LANDS

Subject: Navajo Code Talkers

The **Navajo code talkers** took part in every battle the U.S. Marines conducted in the Pacific from 1942 to 1945, transmitting messages by telephone and radio in their native language, a code that the Japanese never broke.

The idea to use Navajo as a military code came from Philip Johnston, the son of a missionary to the Navajo and one of the few non-Navajo who spoke their language well. Johnston, raised on the Navajo reservation, was a World War I veteran who knew of the military's need for a code that could not be broken.

Johnston believed Navajo would be a perfect code because Navajo is an unwritten language that is very difficult to learn. It has no alphabet or symbols and is spoken only on the Navajo lands of the American Southwest. Some believe that less than 30 non-Navajos could understand the language at the beginning of World War II.

Early in 1942, Johnston met with Major General Clayton B. Vogel and his staff to convince them that Navajo could be used as a code. After several demonstrations, Major Vogel agreed that he was right. In May 1942, the first 29 Navajo recruits attended boot camp. Then, at Camp Pendleton, Oceanside, California, this first group created the Navajo code. They developed a dictionary and numerous words for military terms. The dictionary and all code words had to be memorized during training.

Once Navajo code talkers completed their training, they were sent to a Marine unit in the Pacific. The code talkers' job was to give information about plans, troop movements, orders, and other duties over telephones and radios. They also acted as messengers and performed the jobs all Marines had to do.

The Navajo language confused the Japanese, who were skilled code breakers. Navajo remained valuable as code even after World War II. For that reason, the code talkers, whose skill and courage saved American lives and helped win the war, recently earned recognition from the Federal Government.

NAVAJO CODE TALKERS

PAGE FROM THE NAVAJO CODE
BOOK RELEASED BY THE MILITARY
AFTER WORLD WAR II.

CONFIDENTIAL

NAMES OF ORGANIZATIONS (Con't)

MILITARY MEANING	NAVAJO PRONUNCIATION	NAVAJO MEANING
Battalion	Tachene	Red Soil
Company	Nakia	Mexican
Platoon	Has-clish-nih	Mud
Section	Yo-ih	Beads
Squad	Debeh-li-zini	Black Sheep

COMMUNICATION NAMES

MILITARY MEANING	NAVAJO PRONUNCIATION	NAVAJO MEANING
Telephone	Besh-hal-ne-ih	Telephone
Switchboard	Ya-ih-e-tih-ih	Central
Wire	Besh-le-chee-ih	Copper
Telegraph	Besh-le-chee-ih-beh-hane-ih	Comm by copper wire
Semaphore	Dah-na-a-tah-ih-beh-hane-ih	Flag Signals
Blinker	Coh-nil-kol-lih	Fire Blinder
Radio	Nil-chi-hal-ne-ih	Radio
Panels	At-kad-be-ha-ne-ih	Carpet Signals

OFFICERS NAMES

MILITARY MEANING	NAVAJO PRONUNCIATION	NAVAJO MEANING
Officers	A-la-jih-na-zini	Headmen
Major General	So-na-kih	Two stars
Brigadier General	So-a-la-ih	One star
Colonel	Atsah-besh-le-gai	Silver Eagle
Lt.Colonel	Che-chil-be-tah-besh-legai	Silver Oak Leaf
Major	Che-chil-be-tah-ola	Gold Oak Leaf
Captain	Besh-legai-na-kih	Two Silver Bars
1st Lieutenant	Besh-legai-a-lah-ih	One Silver Bar
2d Lieutenant	Ola-alah-ih-ni-ahi	One Gold Bar

AIRPLANE NAMES

MILITARY MEANING	NAVAJO PRONUNCIATION	NAVAJO MEANING
Airplanes	Wo-tah-de-ne-ih	Air Force
Dive Bomber	Gini	Chicken Hawk
Torpedo Plane	Tas-chizzle	Swallow
Observation Plane	Ne-as-jah	Owl
Fighter Plane	Da-he-tih-hi	Humming Bird
Bomber	Jay-sho	Buzzard
Patrol Plane	Ga-gih	Crow
Transport Plane	Atsah	Eagle

SHIPS NAMES

MILITARY MEANING	NAVAJO PRONUNCIATION	NAVAJO MEANING
Ships	Toh-dineh-ih	Sea Force
Battleship	Lo-tso	Whale
Aircraft Carrier	Tsidi-ney-ye-hi	Bird Carrier
Submarine	Besh-lo	Iron Fish

-2-

CONFIDENTIAL

EARLY
EXPLORERS

EARLY EXPLORERS

ESCALANTE AND DOMÍNGUEZ

The Spanish explorers were the next group to find themselves becoming part of Utah's incredible story. Among the best known of these were Fathers **Francisco Atanasio Domínguez** and **Silvestre Vélez de Escalante.** Father Domínguez was born in Mexico, and Father Escalante was born in Spain. They had both spent a lot of time preaching to the "Indians" in the Mexico area, which today includes Mexico, California, New Mexico, and Arizona.

The two fathers departed Mexico in 1776 with a mission to bring back information about the unexplored northern country. They left Santa Fe on July 29 with a group that included twelve Spanish men and two Ute boys. The boys were from Utah Valley and were brought along to help guide them. The Fathers could not pronounce the young boys' names, so they decided to call them **Silvestre** and **Joaquin.**

In August of 1776, they crossed territory where the Spanish had traveled before. Another Spanish explorer, Muniz, had passed through the region a few years earlier, and Spanish traders

ESCALANTE'S ROUTE

had bartered with the Utes in western Colorado as well. On September 12, the party crossed what would later become the Utah border near what is now Dinosaur National Monument. By this time, they had ventured into lands the Spanish did not know, with Silvestre and Joaquin guiding them.

Following Silvestre and Joaquin toward their homeland in Utah Valley, the party crossed the Green River as well as the Duchesne and Strawberry Rivers. They then crossed from the Uinta Basin into the Diamond Fork area and followed the Spanish Fork River. Upon entering the Utah Valley, they left the river and climbed a hill near what is now the Spanish Oaks Golf Course and wind farm, from which they first saw the entire valley.

As they entered the valley, they quickly determined that this was a location where the Spanish could create a settlement similar to those in the Mexico area. They promised the natives that they would return within a year. They also began looking for a new guide who could continue with them on their quest since Joaquin and Silvestre were going to stay in the valley.

They did manage to recruit another guide, whom they called Jose Maria, to guide them, and they left, heading on a southwestward route. As they reached what is now Milford on October 5th, their guide, Jose Maria, deserted them after being frightened by an argument between some of the men.

At this time it became clear that winter would be there soon. Domínguez and Escalante decided to return to Santa Fe. In trying to return by the quickest way possible, the group found themselves at the edge of the Grand Canyon, peering down at the rugged terrain far below. They eventually found a crossing through what is now Lake Powell's Padre Bay, named for the Spanish word for father, which is *padre*. The group finally arrived in Santa Fe on January 2, 1777, after a journey of over 1,700 miles.

Even though the fathers promised to return and settle the Utah Valley area, because of the distance from their other settlements, they never did. Years later, however, traders and trappers benefited from the trails and maps they left.

ALEXANDER VON HUMBOLDT

A German geographer **Alexander von Humboldt** found the Domínguez-Escalante journals many years later and published some of their maps and findings. **John C. Frémont,**

ALEXANDER
VON HUMBOLDT

a famous American mapmaker, later published detailed maps of the area. Frémont talked about the fathers' journals in his report of the 1843 expedition that he took to Utah. Frémont also named the Spanish Fork River in honor of the two explorers. Frémont's writings later helped the Mormons who read them to learn details of the area and use this information in their travels west.

THE SPANISH TRAIL

The **Spanish Trail** was a major trail between Santa Fe and Los Angeles. It was used for decades by explorers, traders, trappers, and settlers. A large section of the trail curves north through central and southern Utah before bending south again and passing out of the state. The trail was used for slave trading and, in more modern times, an interstate highway.

The Spanish Trail measures 1,120 miles long and passes through New Mexico, Colorado, Utah, Arizona, Nevada, and California. Many people think the Spanish explorers created the trail, but that is not true. Many parts of the trail were well known to the Native Americans, such as the Fremont

OLD SPANISH TRAIL

peoples, long before the Spanish arrived. The trail actually got its name from John C. Frémont, who traveled much of the trail in the 1840s. He had assumed, mostly because of the journals of Escalante and Domínguez, that the route had been laid out by the Spanish, so he named it after them.

The trail enters Utah from the east, near the town of Monticello, and continues northwest near the town of Green River. Northwest of Moab the trail crosses the Colorado River at a spot where low water reveals a small island. The trail eventually crosses the desert until it reaches the Green River, again where an island appears at low water. The trail then travels up the north edge of the San Rafael Swell until it reaches the Black Hills in Emery County. The trail then bends southwest as it crosses the Great Basin, and eventually climbs Holt Canyon, crosses Mountain Meadows, enters the Virgin River Basin, and then moves into Arizona.

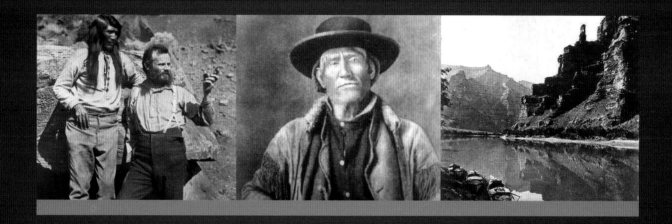

TRAPPERS
AND
TRADERS

JIM BRIDGER

Trappers and traders were also a huge part of Utah's history. Perhaps the most famous of these was **James (Jim) Bridger.** Jim Bridger is often credited as the first European to see the Great Salt Lake, although evidence indicates that others may have found it first. Bridger believed the lake was part of the Pacific Ocean.

JIM BRIDGER

Bridger first entered Utah with a group of trappers and traders in 1824. He spent the next few years in the Utah Valley, trapping and trading with the natives. During the final years of the fur trade, Bridger and his partner, **Pierre Louis Vasquez,** built a fort that is now known as Fort Bridger. This fort was to become one of the main stopping and trading posts for groups of settlers and explorers heading west.

In 1847, Bridger first met the Mormon settlers headed west. He provided them with hand-drawn maps of the area as well as information about the Salt Lake Valley. One story says he expressed to the Mormon leaders his concern about being able to settle the area because of the dry climate. Another suggests he recommended it because of its open grasslands. Whatever the truth, the Mormons decided on Utah.

Bridger later led a number of groups throughout the area, mapping and creating trails. One of the more important trails he created later became the route for the Union Pacific Railroad.

The Mormons purchased Fort Bridger from him in about 1853 for 8,000 dollars. In 1857, the fort was destroyed by the Mormons to slow the march of Albert Sidney Johnston's Army, which was sent to take control of Mormon territory. The army was being guided in their march by none other than Jim Bridger himself. The army occupied the fort for the next few years, in which time Bridger tried to get the fort back, making accusations that the Mormons had stolen the fort from him and kicked him out.

Bridger had a huge impact on the settlement of Utah. His explorations, trails, and maps provided many opportunities for others to enter the area and build Utah into what it is today.

JOHN C. FRÉMONT

John C. Frémont was another explorer who had a tremendous impact on Utah's story. Frémont was well trained in math, science, and surveying. Frémont led five expeditions into Utah. During those expeditions he

JOHN C. FRÉMONT

traveled out onto the Great Salt Lake, studied Utah Lake, and was the first to write about the Great Basin.

Frémont served as the governor of the Arizona Territory from 1878–81. He ran for president in 1856, being the first republican to do so, but lost to James Buchanan. Frémont also served as a commander in the Union Army, under President Abraham Lincoln.

Frémont's greatest achievements were in the area of map-making and publishing. Frémont's maps and accounts of his explorations of the Utah area were key in establishing permanent settlements. They were also used for decades as the best source of accurate information for both settlers and other adventurers.

JOHN WESLEY POWELL

John Wesley Powell was another famous explorer of the area now known as Utah. In 1867 Powell began his explorations of the Rocky Mountains and the Green and Colorado Rivers. His most famous journey took place in 1869, when he and his party made

JOHN WESLEY POWELL

LAKE POWELL

the 900-mile journey down the Green River in Wyoming, through Utah, and into the Grand Canyon. Powell also explored the Utah areas now known as Canyonlands National Park, Grand Staircase-Escalante National Monument, Lake Powell National Recreation Area, Grand Canyon National Park, Bryce Canyon National Park, and Zion National Park.

Powell studied the geology and botany of Utah and the West. He wrote many books on his research. He also studied the Native Americans and their languages. He was one of the first to publish books on the subject.

In addition to his research, Powell was named director of the United States Geological Survey and the Smithsonian Institute's Bureau of Ethnology. He also became a well-known advocate for conserving the natural resources of Utah and the West.

UTAH'S HIDDEN HISTORY

Beavers were trapped for their furs, called pelts. Their pelts were used to make different types of clothing. The most popular item made from beaver pelts was the beaver hat.

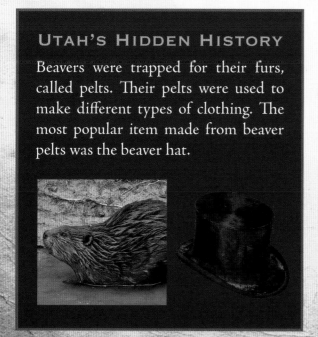

UTAH'S HIDDEN HISTORY

John Wesley Powell had only one arm. His other arm was lost during the Civil War. This makes his accomplishments even more incredible, showing that anything is possible if you have the desire.

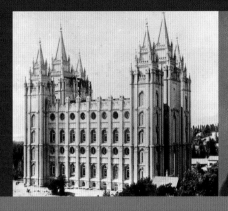

THE
MORMON
PIONEERS

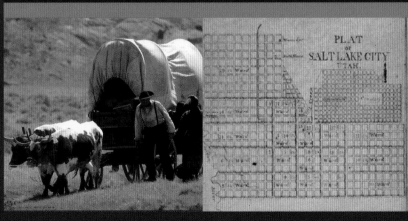

THE MORMON PIONEERS

The **Mormon pioneers** were the next group to enter Utah, and the first since the natives to establish long-term settlements. The term "Mormon" is a nickname given to members of **The Church of Jesus Christ of Latter-day Saints** because of the **Book of Mormon,** which is an additional set of scripture they believe in.

The Mormons ended up in Utah because they were driven out of their homes all over the country. It all started when **Joseph Smith,** the first prophet of the church, translated an ancient record that was called the Book of Mormon, named after the prophet-warrior who had compiled it nearly 2,000 years earlier.

BOOK OF MORMON

The book was published in 1830, and Joseph Smith soon became the target of anger and hatred because of his claims and beliefs.

On April 6, 1830, Smith and five other men organized their church under the name The Church of Christ. The church began using its current name eight years later. Not quite a year after the church was organized, Joseph Smith led most of the Mormons from New York to Ohio, where there was a large number of church members already living.

Members of the church played a major part in developing that area, including creating their own bank. The bank failed because of the national panic of 1837, and this, along with other problems, eventually forced Joseph Smith and **Brigham Young,** one of the most prominent members of the church, to flee for their lives to the state of Missouri.

The Mormons were just as hated in Missouri as they were in Ohio. Their beliefs and their acceptance of free blacks, along with fears that the Mormons would soon take over the local government and banks, led to mob violence, pillaging, and the murder of Mormon settlers. It was at about this time that **Governor Lilburn W.**

MORMON PIONEER REENACTMENT

Boggs issued his infamous **"Extermination Order"** stating that all Mormons must either be driven out of Missouri or be killed. In the winter of 1838–39, they were driven from the state.

The Mormons then moved on to Illinois, where they purchased land and began to build the city of Nauvoo. Joseph Smith eventually became the mayor of Nauvoo, the editor of the local newspaper, and lieutenant general of the **Nauvoo Legion.** He even became a candidate for the president of the United States in 1844.

SALT LAKE TEMPLE

On July 24, 1847, Brigham Young entered the Salt Lake valley. There is much disagreement about the famous statement Young is credited with making, **"This is the right place, drive on,"** but the fact is, they stayed. This was the beginning of the Utah we see today.

It didn't take long for the Mormons to be persecuted in this new city as well. In 1844, Joseph Smith and his brother Hyrum were taken to jail in Carthage, Illinois, and there, on June 27, they were murdered by a mob. After Joseph Smith's death, Brigham Young became the leader of the church.

Because of continued problems and hatred in the area, the Mormons were again forced from their homes. They set out westward, toward what is now Utah. By reading journals and maps from John C. Frémont and other explorers, the Mormon settlers decided that the Salt Lake Valley would be the best location for a new settlement.

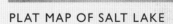

PLAT MAP OF SALT LAKE

THE FIRST COLONIES

Brigham Young sent out groups to other areas to establish colonies in the following years. Thirty families were sent to settle the Utah Valley, fifty families to the Sanpete Valley, and additional families to the Tooele Valley in 1849. The Box Elder, Pahvant, Juab, and Parowan Valleys were then settled in 1851, and the Cache Valley in 1856.

When the Mormon Settlers arrived, Utah was not part of the United States. It had been controlled by Mexico since the Spanish first colonized the area. In March of 1849, Brigham Young and the settlers wanted to become a state. Brigham Young and other leaders created the **State of Deseret,** which, according to the Book of Mormon, means *honeybee.*

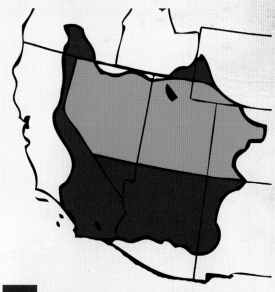

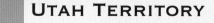

■ **STATE OF DESERET**

■ **UTAH TERRITORY**

The State of Deseret was never recognized by the United States government and only existed for a few years. In 1850, the federal government created the **Utah Territory.** On February 3, 1851, Brigham Young became the first governor of the Utah Territory, and the state of Deseret was no more.

BRIGHAM YOUNG

Brigham Young remained governor of the Utah Territory until 1858. During this time, cities and towns were colonized throughout the territory. Towns and farms were established and flourished as a result of irrigation systems being designed and implemented.

Farming went well in the Salt Lake Valley except in 1848. The legend goes that in that year the crops began to be destroyed by millions of Rocky Mountain crickets. Then suddenly a miracle seemed to occur. Orson F. Whitney, one of the community leaders of the time, said the following, "When it seemed that nothing could stay the devastation, great flocks of gulls appeared, filling the air with their white wings and plaintive cries, and settled down upon the half-ruined fields. All day long they gorged themselves, and when full, disgorged and feasted again, the white gulls upon the black crickets . . . until the pests were vanquished and the people were saved."

After eating the crickets, the gulls returned "to the lake islands whence they came."

The **California gulls,** which inhabit the Great Salt Lake, had come to the rescue. They descended on the fields and devoured thousands of crickets. They helped save the crops and established themselves as a critical part of Utah history. In 1955, the California gull was selected as Utah's state bird.

Because of this incident, as well as droughts in years to come, the settlers did not always have enough food. During those times they turned to other sources of food such as the bulb of the **sego lily,** which was made Utah's state flower in 1911.

UTAH STATE FLAG

SEGO LILY

CALIFORNIA GULL

THE GREAT SALT LAKE

THIS IS THE PLACE MONUMENT

THE
TRANSCONTINENTAL
RAILROAD

THE TRANSCONTINENTAL RAILROAD

COMPLETION OF THE
TRANSCONTINENTAL RAILROAD
MAY 10, 1869

COMMEMORATIVE
STATE QUARTER

As Utah and the West continued to grow, transportation became a problem. The only way to transport goods from states such as California was by wagon. This was a very long process and required traveling through the mountains in poor weather. It also meant that there were many months in the winter when travel was nearly impossible due to the snow and ice.

As the problem became worse, a solution was reached. A **transcontinental railroad,** linking the east and west, was to be constructed. The Union Pacific Railroad Company would build the tracks westward beginning in Iowa, and the Central Pacific Railroad Company would build eastward starting in California.

Construction began in 1863 and continued for six years, until 1869. The Central Pacific Railroad moved much more slowly because of rough mountains and rocky terrain. The Union Pacific Territory was able to move at a much quicker pace and covered more ground because they were working in the flat plains of the midwestern United States.

THE GOLDEN SPIKE

On May 8, 1869, the two groups met at **Promontory Summit (Point), Utah.** Two days later on May 10, to celebrate the event, a golden spike was driven into the tracks. The golden spike was made of 17-karat copper-alloyed gold and weighed 14.03 troy ounces. It

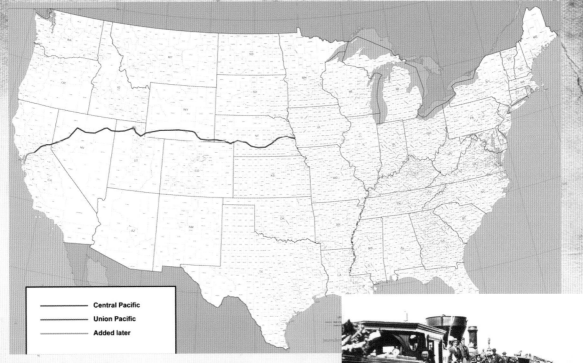

TRANSCONTINENTAL RAILROAD ROUTE

Central Pacific
Union Pacific
Added later

was dropped into a pre-drilled hole in the ceremonial last tie, and gently tapped into place with a silver ceremonial hammer. The spike was engraved on all four sides.

made from the laurel tree that produced the final tie on the transcontinental railroad.

THE GOLDEN SPIKE

SIDE 1: The Pacific Railroad ground broken January 8, 1863, and completed May 8, 1869.

SIDE 2: Directors of the C. P. R. R. of Cal. Hon. Leland Stanford. C. P. Huntington. E. B. Crocker. Mark Hopkins. A. P. Stanford. E. H. Miller Jr.

SIDE 3: Officers. Hon. Leland Stanford. Presdt. C. P. Huntington Vice Presdt. E. B. Crocker. Atty. Mark Hopkins. Tresr. Chas Crocker Gen. Supdt. E. H. Miller Jr. Secty. S. S. Montague. Chief Engr.

SIDE 4: May God continue the unity of our Country, as this Railroad unites the two great Oceans of the world. Presented by David Hewes San Francisco.

THE
QUEST
FOR
STATEHOOD

TROUBLE IN WASHINGTON

As a result of the railroad, settlers poured west like never before. All of the western areas, including Utah, grew at a rate that had never been seen. They had been trying to become a state for decades with no success, but that was soon to change.

After Brigham Young had held the office of governor for nearly eight years, the federal government began to worry. They did not agree with many of the beliefs of the Mormon leaders and decided to take control of the territory.

Just after taking office in 1857, President Buchanan removed Brigham Young as governor of the Utah Territory and sent a 2,500-man military force to put in place a new governor, **Alfred Cumming.** When the military finally made it to Salt Lake City on June 26, 1858, they found it abandoned by the Mormons. Cumming became governor without a fight and eventually made peace with the Mormons.

Utah continued to petition the federal government for statehood. Each time they got close, their efforts would fail, including in 1862 when the Morrill Anti-Bigamy Act of the Senate disincorporated (broke up) the Mormon church. This act was never implemented, however, and the church remained intact.

For many more years, Utah would apply for statehood. The struggle did not get easier. In fact it seemed to those in the territory that every time Utah would apply for statehood, not only were they not made a state, but the Mormon church and the territory were punished. The U.S. Senate passed the Edmunds-Tucker bill on January 12, 1886, and President Cleveland allowed it to become law without his signature. This act stated that property of the Mormon church worth more than 50,000 dollars total must be given to the United States. The bill also took away the right for women to vote in the territory.

A NEW CONSTITUTION

On March 4, 1895, Utah leaders met in the new Salt Lake City and County Building and wrote Utah's new constitution. The group was made up of a mix of Mormons and non-Mormons from a wide range of backgrounds. They finished writing the constitution, and signed it on May 8. During the general election on November 5, 1895, the new constitution was ratified, and state officials and state legislators were elected. Again a petition was sent to the federal government for Utah to become a state.

On January 4, 1896, President Cleveland proclaimed Utah a state. The long struggle for statehood was over.

Utah officially became the forty-fifth state in

SALT LAKE CITY AND COUNTY BUILDING

TERRITORIAL STATEHOUSE IN FILLMORE, UTAH

the Union. **Heber Manning Wells** became the first governor of the State of Utah. At this same time, Utah again gave women the right to vote, becoming one of the first states to do so.

A CAPITOL CRISIS

As Utah tried to become a state, it needed a capitol. **Fillmore, Utah** had served as the territory capitol from 1851–56. This location was chosen because the state legislature felt the capitol should be near the center of the state. During this time, the federal government had given Utah money to build a capitol building, and the **Utah Territorial Statehouse** was constructed. The statehouse can still be visited in Fillmore to this day.

However, in the course of Utah's battle for statehood, the territorial leaders decided that Fillmore was not where the capitol should be. They only held one full legislative session in the new statehouse before deciding it was time to move. At this point they decided to relocate the capitol to the original city founded by the Mormons, **Salt Lake City.** Salt Lake City became the state capitol of the newly formed state and remains the capitol to this day.

TERRITORY AND STATE RIGHTS	TERRITORY	STATE
Residents can vote for President of the United States	NO	YES
Elected representatives in Congress	NO	YES
Can create local laws	FEW	YES

Salt Lake City gets its name from the Great Salt Lake, which sits on its western side. Explorers at times mistook the lake for part of the Pacific Ocean because of the salt water it contains. The Great Salt Lake is all that remains of the once great Lake Bonneville. It is the largest lake in Utah, and one of the largest in the United States. As water in the mountains above the lake dissolves minerals, they flow to the lake. Once there, because there is no way for the water to get out, it evaporates and leaves behind only salt and minerals. This causes the lake to be very salty.

With the new capitol in place, there was a problem. The statehouse was still located in Fillmore. Utah again asked the federal government for funds to assist in building a new capitol building. This time they were told no. It was left to those living in Utah to come up with a way to pay for the new building, which they knew would be very expensive.

In the 1909 legislative session, three bills were passed that would help pay for the construction of the building. At the same time, A.R. Barnes, Utah's attorney general, found a state inheritance tax in the Utah law that was not being used. He decided to enforce this law for the estate of E.H. Harriman, a man who had made millions with the railroad. This resulted in nearly eight-hundred thousand dollars that could be used for the building. The legislature

also passed a bill that allowed them to get a loan of nearly two million dollars. With this money, they had enough to begin the project.

The state legislature then began asking for designs to be submitted. They would look over these designs and select the one that they felt best represented Utah and would serve as an icon. The legislature eventually chose Richard Kletting's plan, which was similar to the United States Capitol building. Construction began in 1912 and finished in 1916.

The granite that makes up most of the building was taken from nearby Little Cottonwood Canyon. The large dome in the center is covered with copper that came from the mountains of Utah. If you look on both the outside and inside of the building, you will find countless beehives carved into stone and cast in metal. This was done to represent cooperation and industry.

UTAH'S HIDDEN HISTORY

Copper is Utah's state mineral. In 1994, the Utah State legislature passed a bill making copper the state mineral because of its many important uses.

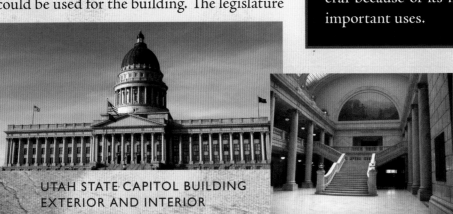

UTAH STATE CAPITOL BUILDING
EXTERIOR AND INTERIOR

SYMBOLS TO LOOK FOR IN THE UTAH STATE CAPITOL BUILDING AND THEIR MEANINGS

ACANTHUS — Tree and leaves stand for overcoming life's trials.

BEE — Diligence, organization, cooperation, wisdom, courage, creativity, selflessness, and illumination.

CIRCLE — Perfection, unity, eternity.

CORNUCOPIA — "Horn of Plenty"—abundance, prosperity, and good luck.

EAGLE — Power, speed, majesty, victory, valor, and inspiration.

EGG — Birth and promise.

LIONS — Authority, courage, wisdom, justice, and protection.

PENTACLE — Five-point star—perfect harmony, strength, and power. Pointing up means a plea for heavenly guidance, pointing down means heaven's attention to the proceedings.

PINE CONE — Spring and rebirth.

POLE STAR — Six- or eight-point star—constancy and dependability.

POMEGRANATE — Unity: many are stronger than one when bound by law.

RAM — Solar energy and fire.

ROSE — Eternal life, the heart, wisdom.

SQUARE — Permanence, security, balance, morality.

WYVERN — A creature with head and paws of a lion or dragon, wings of an eagle, and a serpent's tail. Guardian figure.

BEEHIVE

WYVERN

LION AND PENTACLE

LION

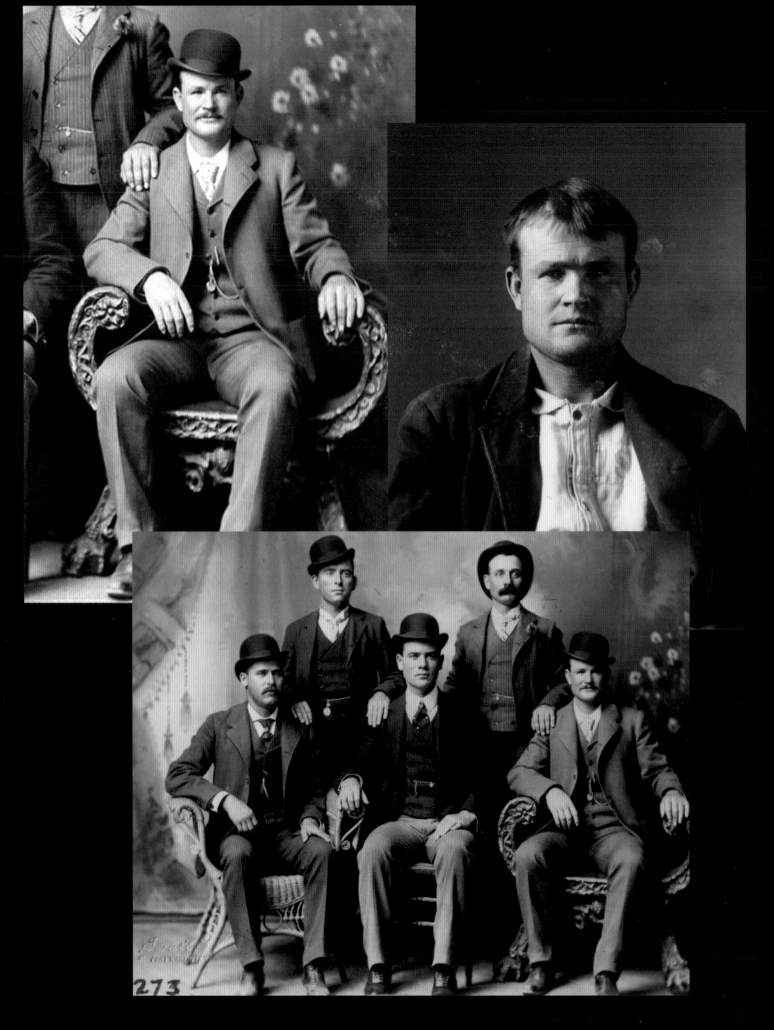

FAMOUS
UTAHNS

With Utah as a state and the new capitol building constructed, we can take a look at some of the famous people who helped make Utah what it is today. We will begin with an individual who was considered a hero by some but an outlaw by most, **Robert LeRoy Parker,** better known as **Butch Cassidy.**

BUTCH CASSIDY

Parker was born in Beaver, Utah, on April 13, 1866. He was the oldest of thirteen children and grew up on his parents' ranch near Circleville. Parker left home in his early teens to find work. He ended up on a dairy farm and became friends with a horse thief and cattle rustler named Mike Cassidy. While working on various farms and ranches, Parker was given the nickname "Butch." To this he added the last name of Cassidy in honor of his good friend and mentor Mike. Thus, the name **"Butch Cassidy"** was born.

BUTCH CASSIDY AND THE WILD BUNCH

It is rumored that Butch Cassidy's life of crime began as a mistake. The story goes that around 1880, he made a journey to a clothing shop in a neighboring town only to find the shop closed. He entered the shop and took a pair of jeans, leaving a note stating that he would pay for them during his next visit. Supposedly, the owner of the clothing store took down the details, which Cassidy had included in the note, and reported him to the sheriff. After explaining the incident to the judge, he was not found guilty of the charges, and he was allowed to pay for the pants and go free.

As things would later turn out, Cassidy did not always live such an honest life. He put together a gang he called the **Wild Bunch** and began robbing banks and trains throughout the west. Cassidy's gang used a hideout in southeastern Utah called **Robbers' Roost** to make their plans and to hide from the law.

Eventually the law closed in on Cassidy and his gang. Many of them were hunted down and killed. As for the famous leader of the gang, there are many rumors as to what really happened to him. One of these is that he and his partner, the Sundance Kid, fled to South America and continued their streak of robberies. It is said that on November 3, 1908, near San Vicente in southern Bolivia,

a deliveryman for a silver mine was carrying his company's payroll when he was attacked and robbed by two Americans. The bandits then proceeded to San Vicente, where they stayed. Three nights later, on November 6, a small group made up of the local mayor, some of his officials, and two soldiers surrounded their house. It was not long until a gunfight broke out.

When the fighting ended, the men entered the house and found two dead bodies, both with numerous gunshot wounds. Both bodies were taken to the local cemetery where they were buried close to the grave of a German miner named Gustav Zimmer. Although attempts have been made to find their unmarked graves, no remains with DNA matching the living relatives of Butch Cassidy or the Sundance Kid have yet been found.

BUTCH CASSIDY

COMPARE THE PHOTOGRAPHS BELOW AND SEE IF YOU THINK BUTCH CASSIDY AND WILLIAM T. PHILLIPS OR THE SUNDANCE KID AND HIRAM BEBEE WERE THE SAME PEOPLE.

WHAT DO YOU THINK?

WANTED
DEAD OR ALIVE

BUTCH CASSIDY

WILLIAM T. PHILLIPS

THE SUNDANCE KID

HIRAM BEBEE

Some people believe that William T. Phillips, the author of *The Bandit Invincible, A Biography of the Outlaw Butch Cassidy* was, in fact, Butch Cassidy. Phillips claimed to have known Cassidy since childhood and seemed to know almost too much about the outlaw. However, there is little evidence to support the claim.

Cassidy's sister, Lula Parker Betenson, stated that he returned alive to the United States and lived under another name for years. In her biography *Butch Cassidy, My Brother*, Betenson tells of several times when people familiar with Butch Cassidy met with him long after 1908, and she relates a detailed description of a "family reunion" with Cassidy, their brother Mark, their father, and herself in 1925.

Another story told by Francis Smith, M.D. is that he saw Butch Cassidy and that Cassidy told Smith his face had been altered by a surgeon in Paris. He also said that Cassidy showed him a repaired bullet wound that Smith recognized as work he had previously done on Cassidy.

There are also reports of the Sundance Kid living in Spring City under the assumed name of Hiram Bebee. The story goes that in 1945, Bebee was causing trouble at a bar in Mt. Pleasant. Marshal Lon Larsen was called and physically removed Bebee from the bar. The marshal tossed him into his own pickup truck, but once he was inside the cab, Bebee grabbed his gun and shot the officer dead. He was convicted of murder and sentenced to death, serving his time at the Utah state penitentiary. The sentence was later changed to life in prison. The only problem with this story is that the Sundance Kid was said to be around 6 feet tall, and Bebee was only around five and a half feet tall, though their photographs do look very similar.

MARTHA MARIA HUGHES CANNON

Our next star, **Martha Maria Hughes Cannon,** was born July 1, 1857 near Llandudno, Wales. In a much-publicized election, Martha was one of five Democrats from Salt Lake County running for state senator. Among the Republicans running against her was her husband, Angus. On November 3, 1896, she won the election, becoming the first woman ever elected

MARTHA MARIA HUGHES CANNON

to that office in the United States. She served two terms in the legislature and was particularly involved with public health issues.

PHILO T. FARNSWORTH

When we think of television, we may not always think of Utah, but the very first television came from right here within our great state. **Philo T. Farnsworth** was born in Beaver, Utah, on April 19, 1906. Not long after his birth, the Farnsworth family moved to Idaho, where they lived in a house that had

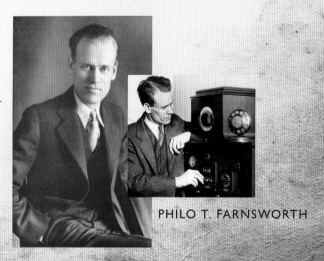

PHILO T. FARNSWORTH

electricity. This was an inspiration to young Philo. Farnsworth soon converted a washing machine from hand to electric power by building an electric motor and connecting it to the cranking arm.

In 1926, he formed a partnership with George Everson in Salt Lake City to develop Farnsworth's television ideas. By 1928, Farnsworth had developed the system sufficiently to hold a demonstration for the press. Those who had given him money are reported to have asked when they would see dollars from the invention. In response, the first image Farnsworth showed to them over the TV was a dollar sign. In 1929 the television system was improved and no longer had mechanical moving parts. That same year, Farnsworth transmitted the first live human images using his television system, including a three-and-a-half-inch image of his wife, Elma (Pem). To this day, many of Farnsworth's technologies and ideas are still used.

JEDEDIAH S. SMITH

JEDEDIAH S. SMITH

Our next spotlight shines upon a trapper named **Jedediah S. Smith**. Smith played a huge part in the exploration of Utah before it became a state. In scouting for good trapping areas, Smith traveled the entire length of Utah, along the route of present-day Interstate 15 to Spanish Fork Canyon, where he crossed into the Sanpete Valley to trade with the Ute Indians.

What makes Smith stand out is that he was the first to cross overland to California, the first to travel the length of Utah, the first to traverse the Sierra Nevada, and the first to cross the Great Basin Desert.

OLD EPHRAIM

Our next individual is very different from the others. He actually became the target of trappers and hunters. **Old Ephraim** is thought to have been the last grizzly to live in the state of Utah. Old Ephraim is one of only a few wild animals anywhere in the United States to have a monument built over his grave. According to some, he was truly one of the largest grizzly bears to ever live.

There are a lot of myths and stories about Old Ephraim, but we will share the story of the man who hunted him down and killed him, Frank Clark. Frank's story is told on the following page.

OLD EPHRAIM'S MONUMENT

OLD EPHRAIM'S SKULL

Old Ephraim

On August 21, 1923, I visited the trap and he (Old Ephraim) had drummed the wallow into a newly built one, so I carefully changed the trap to his newly built bath. I was camped one mile down the canyon in a tent. That night was fine, beautiful, a starlit night, and I was sleeping fine when I was awakened by a roar and a groan near camp. I had a dog, but not a sound came from Mr. Dog. I tried to get to sleep, but no chance; so I got up and put on my shoes but no trousers. I did take my gun, a .25–35 cal. carbine with seven steel ball cartridges, and walked up the trail.

GRIZZLY BEAR

I did not know it was "Eph;" in fact, I thought it was a horse that was down. "Eph" was in the creek in some willows and after I had got past him, he let me know all at once that it was not a horse. What should I do? Alone, the closest human being three miles away and "Eph" between me and camp.

I listened and could hear the chain rattle and so did my teeth. I decided to get up on the hillside and wait for him. I spent many hours up there—I had no way of knowing how many—listening to "Eph's" groans and bellows. Daylight came at last and now it was my turn.

"Eph" was pretty well hidden in the creek bottom and willows, so I threw sticks in to scare him out. He slipped out and went down by the tent and crawled into the willows there. I tracked him down there, and when I got close to the tent, I could see a small patch of hide. I fired at it and grazed the shoulder. Now for me to get the greatest thrill of my life.

"Ephraim" raised up on his hind legs with his back to me, and a 14-foot-long log chain wound around his right arm as carefully as a man would have done it, and a 23-pound bear trap on his foot, standing 9 feet, 11 inches tall. He could have gone that way and have gotten away, but he turned around, and I saw the most magnificent sight that any man could ever see. I was paralyzed with fear and could not raise my gun.

He was coming, still on his hind legs, holding that cussed trap above his head. He had a four foot band to surmount before he could reach me. I was rooted to the earth and let him come within six feet of me before I stuck the gun out and pulled the trigger. He fell back, but came again and received five of the remaining six bullets. He had now reached the trail, still on his hind legs. I only had one cartridge left in the gun and still that bear would not go down.

I started for Logan, 20 miles downhill. I went about 20 yards and turned. "Eph" was coming, still standing up, but my dog was snapping at his heels, so he turned on the dog. I then turned back, and as I got close, he turned again on me, wading along on his hind legs. I could see that he was badly hurt, as at each breath the blood would spurt from his nostrils, so I gave him the last bullet in the brain. I think I felt sorry I had to do it.

Frank Clark, "Thots and Things: Here's the story of Old Ephraim by the man who bagged him," *Herald Journal*, February 24, 1953.

JOHN M. BROWNING

Next on our list is the famous American gun-maker **John M. Browning.** Browning was born in Ogden in January of 1855. Browning's inventions have, in a very real way, changed the world we live in. He is considered the father of automatic weapons, such as machine guns, that are used by the military throughout the world to this day.

Among Browning's most famous inventions were the Colt 1911, the Browning 1917, and the Browning Automatic Rifle (BAR), all of which were used by United States troops in

JOHN M. BROWNING

World War I, World War II, and the Korean War, with the 1911 being used as the United States' standard military side arm until the 1980s. The Browning Hi-Power was just as vital and remains the standard sidearm of the United Kingdom's and Australia's armed forces. The M2 heavy machine gun is also still commonly used throughout the world.

Perhaps the single most infamous Browning gun was an FN Model 1910 handgun, serial number 19074. In 1914, Gavrilo Princip used the pistol to assassinate Archduke Franz Ferdinand of Austria and his wife, Sophie. This event is thought to be the major incident that sparked World War I.

EDWIN JAKE GARN

Utah was also home to the first government leader in the United States to travel into space. On April 12, 1985, the **Space Shuttle Discovery** launched from its pad in Florida. The shuttle was carrying a seven-member crew, which included Utah's Senator **Edwin Jacob (Jake) Garn.**

Garn was a former Brigadier General in the Utah Air National Guard, where he flew fighter jets and other aircraft. After retiring from the National Guard, Garn was elected Mayor of Salt Lake City. Then in 1974, he was elected to the senate and re-elected in 1980, receiving over 70 percent of the vote, one of the highest percentages in Utah history.

On his shuttle mission, Jake Garn orbited the earth for 6 days, 23 hours, and 55 minutes. He orbited the earth 109 times and traveled over 2.5 million miles. He performed many medical tests as part of his mission. On April 19, 1985, the space shuttle touched down after completing its nearly seven-day mission.

SPACE SHUTTLE DISCOVERY

EDWIN JAKE GARN

UTAH'S HIDDEN HISTORY

During his seven-day journey into space, Senator Jake Garn experienced extreme space sickness. He was so sick that NASA created a scale to measure space sickness and named its measurement after him. "One Garn" is the very highest level of space sickness.

FAMOUS UTAHNS

Some of the more prominent people who were born in the state of Utah, live in Utah, or for whom Utah is a significant part of their identity:

MAURICE ABRAVANEL music director of the Utah Symphony for over 30 years.

MAUDE ADAMS Broadway stage actress of the late 19th and early 20th centuries, noted for her title role in Peter Pan.

DAVID ARCHULETA singer-songwriter and runner-up on the seventh season of *American Idol*.

BRUCE BASTIAN cofounder of the WordPerfect software company, philanthropist, member of the board of directors of the Human Rights Campaign.

ROBERT FOSTER "BOB" BENNETT Republican United States Senator from Utah.

EZRA TAFT BENSON 13th President of The Church of Jesus Christ of Latter-day Saints from 1985 to 1994; United States Secretary of Agriculture under Eisenhower.

KURT BESTOR composer, arranger, and performer.

DON BLUTH animator.

MARIO CAPECCHI Nobel Prize laureate for Medicine, 2007.

ORSON SCOTT CARD science fiction author.

STEPHEN COVEY author, *The Seven Habits of Highly Effective People*.

RICHARD PAUL EVANS author best known for his novel *The Christmas Box*.

HENRY EYRING internationally noted theoretical chemist who proposed theories on which future Nobel Prize winners based their work.

JOHN D. FITZGERALD author of *The Great Brain* series of children's books and *Papa Married a Mormon*, describing his Utah roots.

BRANDON FLOWERS singer for the rock band The Killers.

ORRIN HATCH U.S. Senator from Utah.

ARNOLD FRIBERG artist known for his religious and political paintings. He completed 15 "pre-visualization" paintings for the Cecil B. DeMille film *The Ten Commandments*.

GORDON B. HINCKLEY 15th President of The Church of Jesus Christ of Latter-day Saints from 1995 to 2008.

JON HUNTSMAN, JR. Governor of Utah 2005–09; ambassador to the People's Republic of China.

JON HUNTSMAN, SR. businessman, philanthropist, founder of Huntsman Corporation.

KEN JENNINGS 74-time *Jeopardy!* champion.

JEWEL singer-songwriter, guitarist, actress, and poet.

THOMAS KEARNS U.S. Senator from Utah, owned the Silver King Coalition Mine in Park City and the *Salt Lake Tribune*, Utah's largest newspaper.

DAVID M. KENNEDY Treasury Secretary under Nixon.

SPENCER W. KIMBALL LDS President who ended the ban on priesthood for African-Americans in 1978.

MICHAEL O. LEAVITT former Governor of the State of Utah, Secretary of Health and Human Services.

KARL MALONE professional basketball player (retired); two-time NBA MVP, regarded as one of the best power forwards of all time.

JOHN WILLARD MARRIOTT founder of worldwide hotel business Marriott International, Inc.

LARRY H. MILLER businessman, philanthropist, former owner of Utah Jazz basketball team.

GERALD R. MOLEN Academy Award–winning film producer.

THOMAS S. MONSON Current President of The Church of Jesus Christ of Latter-day Saints.

JIM NANTZ CBS Sports anchor.

NEON TREES ROCK BAND from Provo, Utah.

THE OSMOND FAMILY MUSIC GROUP

- **ALAN OSMOND** singer.
- **DONNY OSMOND** singer, actor, television host.
- **JIMMY OSMOND** singer, actor, businessman.
- **MARIE OSMOND** singer, actress, television host.
- **MERRILL OSMOND** singer.
- **JAY OSMOND** singer.
- **WAYNE OSMOND** singer.

ROBERT REDFORD actor, director, movie producer, philanthropist, founder of the Sundance Film Festival.

BRANDON SANDERSON fantasy author.

JERRY SLOAN Hall of Fame head coach for the Utah Jazz; longest-tenured coach in American professional sports, and one of the winningest coaches in NBA history.

ELIZABETH SMART girl kidnapped from her bedroom in Salt Lake City in 2002.

JOHN STOCKTON Hall of Fame point guard for the Utah Jazz, holds the NBA record for career assists and steals.

PICABO STREET champion alpine ski racer with the U.S. Ski Team.

OLENE S. WALKER governor.

LORETTA YOUNG Motion-picture actress.

MAHONRI YOUNG Sculptor and artist.

STEVE YOUNG Hall of Fame quarterback for the San Francisco 49ers, NFL MVP 1992 and 1994.

"All Gave Some - Some Gave All"

Japanese-American U.S. veterans who served their country despite the fact that almost all were incarcerated at Topaz.

* Killed in action

Nisei U.S. veterans listing courtesy Veterans Memorial of Fillmore. All listed Nisei veterans lived at one time in Millard County

WWI Veterans
Kotaro Tsukamoto
N. Sasaki

WWII Veterans
Chester Abe
Larry Adkawa
Han Assau
K. Akagi
James Akashi
George Aki
Bert Akiyama
Hiromo Asai
Shiro Asahina
Paul Amano
Roy Ashizawa
Yuki Ashizawa
Junji Deane
Frank Dobashi
Shozo Deiguchi
Walter Fujima
Minoru Endo
Norio Endo
Sam Fujikawa
Henry Fukui
George Fukui
taishi Furudno,
Ace Furuta
Jun Furuya
jitsu Furuya
taishi Futagaki
Jiro Hada
Dan Hamachi
Isamoto
Harada
Harada
Harada
Hata
Hata
oyoshi
di

Henry Hidekawa
Nobuto Hidenhima
Tad Hikenuda
Kiyoshi Hirano
Roy Hirano
Jackson Hirose
Norman Hirose
Kiku Hirowatsu
Henry Honda
Shoji Horikawa
Robert Honhino
Haruo Ichiyasu
Joe Igatochi
S. Iijima
Edwin Iino
William Iino
Roy Ikeda
Sam Ikeda
Mas Imada
Heiyu Imai
Tomo Inaba
Joe Inatomi
Eddie Ino
Mas Ishida
Joe Ishitaki
Mas Inobe
Yukio Inoda
Tom Inohashi
Hisashi Iwai
Setsomu Iwase
Seiji Kaibe

* Nobuo Kajiwara
Frank Kami
Yoneoso Kamakluta
Wataru Kameya
* James Kanada
Alice Karagaki
Miyoshi Karasaki
Million Karisaki
Sekio Kansaki
Takaaki Kashima
Saburo Katayama
Taro Katayama
Henry Kato
* John Kato
Joseph Kato
Kazuo Kato
Tsu Kato
Ben Kawaguchi
Katsumi Kawaguchi
Keyino Kawaguchi
Masaru Kawaguchi
Tadayuki Kawaguchi
Effie Kawahara
Thomas Kawahara
Jack Kawakami
Jim Kawakami
Joseph Kawamura
Shigeru Kawamoto
George Kayano
Shigeru Kayano
Kijoichi Keikoan

Al Kimoto
Jim Kimoto
Tad Kimoto
Frank Kimura
Joe Kimura
Rusty Kinosta
Sam Kinoshita
Jim Kirihara
Jiro Kishi
George Kitagawa
Mimoto Kitagawa
Peter Kitagawa
Saburo Kitagawa
Tamiji Kitagawa
Kino Kitamura
Tomio Kitamura
Tyler Nakamura
Yutaka Kitsutani
Chiaki Kojimo
Nobuo Kono
Kingo Kotake
Kiyoshi Kusunoki
Koneo Maruyama
Ken Matsuda
Frank Matsui
George Matsui
Isamie Matsukawa
Joe Matsuki
Paul Matsumi
Frank Matsumoto
George Matsumoto
Masakichi Matsuzaki
Kiyoshi Midzuno
Yosh Mihara
Timothy Minokami
Tak Minami
* Tom Minami
M. Minutani
Jack Mizono
Earl Mizote
Henry Mizore
Bill Mizuno
John Mizuno
Vincent Momii

Kazuo Mori
Hubuto Moriguchi
Art Morimoto
Ginzo Morino
Kenji Morino
Walton Morita
Aki Moriwaki
Fred Murakami
Tokio Murakami
Bill Moriasuto
Mas Nagasawa
William Nakahara Jr.
Hirokazu Nakai
George Nakamura
Jim Nakamura
Tyler Nakamura
Jim Nakano
Hisashi Nakao
Mincru Nakayama
Shig Nakayama
Tomio Nakayama
Tyler Nakayama
Makoto Nao
Hideso Nenshi
Ken Nihei
Hiroshi Nishikubo
Raymond Nomura
Henry Obayashi
Shitotoshi Ochi
Somao Ochi
Tetsuo Ochi
Agnes Ogi
Bill Ogo
Hirozaka Okada
James Okada
* James Okamoto
Toru Okamoto
Teiji Okuda
Teiko Okuda
Yuki Okuda
Frank Okuto
Hiroshi Onishi
John Oshima
* Daniel Ota

Kenji Ota
Mincru Ota
Tahara Ota
Akira Otsuki
Shizuo Osaki
Koji Osawa
Masumi Sado
Tatsumasa Saginori
* Tom Sagimori
Leo Saito
Masaaki Sakaguchi
Bill Sakai
Hisaji Sakai
Tomio Sakurai
Hisanori Sano
Yukio Sano
Sekio Sasaki
Naoharu Satake
Ned Satake
Michael Sato
York Sato
George Sera
Eichi Shibata
Matt Shigio
Kensomi Shikano
Roy Shimada
Kenichi Shimomura
Harry Shin
John Shinagawa
Kiyoshi Shimomimi
Shigeomi Shiovishi
Takao Sonoda
Chuji Sowa
* Hiroshi Sugiyama
Tsutomu Sumimoto
William Suyeyasu
Ken Suzuki
* Tetsuo Tabara
James Taiji
Tatsumi Tajima
Wally Takaguchi
Chikara Takaha
Santui Takaha
Yoneji Takaha
Shigeharu Takahashi

James Takaki
Paul Takara
Shogi Takata
Tadao Takayanagi
Taru Takeda
Shuji Takei
Shizuo Takera
Masakjiro Taketomi
Ichiro Takeuchi
Shoyi Takimure
Jiry Tamaki
John Tamaki
Osamu Tamaki
Satoshi Tamura
Toshiya Tamura
Harry Tanabe
Kiyoshi Tanamachi
Paul Tani
Jiow Taniguchi
Tsunemo Tatsutno
Kaz Tawa
James Toda
Sam Tominaga
Tom Tomioka
Joe Tordo
John Toritomi
Stanley Tsujiaaka
Himeo Tsumori
* Isao Tsuno
Khyuhi Uheromiya
Osji Wayamima
John Wada
Mas Yago
George Yaki
Masao Yamamoto
William Yamamoto
George Yamasaki
Motoichi Yanagi
Arthur Yano
Frank Yano
George Yano
Lee Yano
Warren Yano
Joe Yasuda
Hitoshi Yonekura
Satoshi Yonekura

Alex Yorichi
Ronald Yoshida
Kiyoshi Yoshii
Tad Yoshii
Mike Yoshimine
Joe Yoshines
John Yoshino
Paul Yoshino
Tom Yoshitome

Korean Veterans
Seiji Ainawa
Peter Asano
Tadashi Asano
Takane Eshima
Nobusuke Fukuda
Salvito Fukuda
Paul Fukui
Bill Hirose
Sei Hirose
Hidemaro S. Ishida
Yukio Isoye
Ken Ito

Tak Iwamoto
Nob Iwasa
Stanley Karosaki
HiJ Kashima
Hartap Kato
Masao Kato
Toshino Katsura
Joe Kawakami
Daniel Kawamoeta
Mikio Kirihara
Chuck Kubokawa
Kiyoshi Kurimubo
Edward Matsui
Hirofumi Miyachi
Bill Mizono
Albert Minahara
Shigeru Morita
Mas Naguzawa
Donald Nakahara
Edward Nakata
Isamu Nao
Frank Nishioka
Kinzio Okinewichi
John Oshima

Tomio Ozawa
Adachi Sachi
Ken Sato
Mike Sato
Arthur Serata
Henry Serata
Walter Serata
Keiji Shibata
James Shidawara
Sam Shimomura
Yuichi Sumi
Tom Suyeyama
Mikko Suzuki
Yas Suzuki
Edwin Takahashi
Shin Tanaka
Jack Tsuboi
Takenori Tsuchiya
Bob Utsumi
Arthur Uyeda
Keiguo Yamasaki
Taka Yoshida

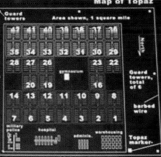

★ John Harano

442nd Regimental Combat Team, 100th Infantry Battalion, Military Intelligence Service (MIS)

Formed during WWII, these three US Military units were comprised of Japanese-American young men from the US mainland, Hawaii and from ten internment camps such as Topaz. Despite heated racial attitudes, many young men volunteered to show their loyalty to their country. Their valor and fighting spirit became known throughout the US military. The rescue of the Lost Battalion in France typified their bravery - in fierce combat they suffered huge casualties (199 KIA or missing, hundreds wounded in action) while rescuing 211 men of the Texas Battalion. During the war they received over 16,000 decorations to become the most decorated unit for its size and length of service in military history. However, only a single Congressional Medal of Honor was given due to racial overtones. This was corrected in 2000 when President Clinton upgraded 20 Distinguished Cross Medals to Congressional Medal of Honor awards to Japanese-American veterans, many of whom were in their Some were given posthumously.

You are here

GO FOR BROKE

Map of Topaz

Guard towers   Area shown, 1 square mile

42	41	40	39	38	37	36
35	34	33	32	31	30	29
28	27	26			23	22
	20	19		16		
14	13	12	11	10	9	8
7	6	5	4	3	2	1

gymnasium

Guard towers, total of 6

barbed wire

military police   hospital   admin.   warehousing

Topaz marker

highway

＿Ｚ INTERNMENT CAMP

...rds of whom are U.S. citizens, are ...ncarcerated by their own government. ...ey are imprisoned in ten inland ...hind barbed wire, under suspicion ...z is one of the ten camps. ☐ Without ...d solely on the color of their skin ...r and distrust of these citizens— ...rbor—is placated. ☐ Lost within ...nal rights, major losses of personal ...as enemy. Ironically, though this ...s of disloyalty, not a single case of ... ☐ Indeed, the 442nd RCT and ...apanese-American boys (many of ...r major war casualties and go on ...ed combat unit in its history. ☐ ...ry of Topaz remains a tribute to a ...while America's had faltered.

Gold star mothers, incarcerated behind barbed wire, welcome home their U.S. veteran sons— while at the same time, mourn for sons lost, fighting for America.

Above:
Internee messhall

Left:
Third grade class

Right:
Young internee family

WAR
AND
CONFLICT

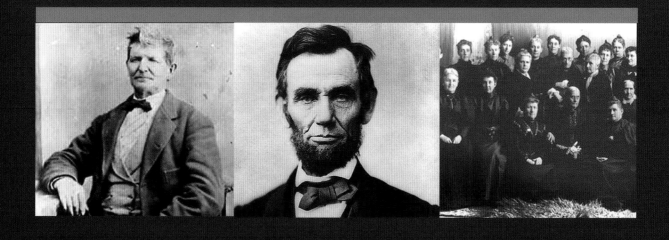

WAR AND CONFLICT

THE UTAH WAR

Utah has also been the center for a number of wars that have helped to shape the state. The **Utah War** was largely based on misunderstandings and a lack of information on the part of the federal government. From 1857 to 1858, President Buchanan tried to end what he saw as a rebellion in Utah Territory. Buchanan dispatched a large federal army to the territory, possibly to kill the Mormons. To slow the advancing army, the Mormons blocked the entrance into the Salt Lake Valley. While the confrontation between the Mormon militia, called the Nauvoo Legion, and the U.S. Army involved some destroyed property and a few small battles in what is today southwestern Wyoming, major fighting did not take place.

THE MOUNTAIN MEADOWS MASSACRE

At the height of the conflict, on September 11, 1857, over 120 settlers traveling from Arkansas to California—including unarmed men, women, and children—were killed in southwestern Utah by a group of local Mormon militiamen, possibly with the help of Paiute allies. This tragic event was later called the **Mountain Meadows Massacre.** While this incident was probably connected to the hysteria surrounding the approaching federal army, which invaded Utah in 1857, two major theories exist on why the leader of the group, **John D. Lee,** committed such an act.

MONUMENT AT MOUNTAIN MEADOWS

JOHN D. LEE

The first is that Brigham Young, acting through other Mormon leaders, ordered him to commit this act. There is little evidence to support this theory, however. The more probable theory is that he acted under his own direction. This is evident in several letters written shortly after the terrible event. He had written a letter to Brigham Young shortly after the massacre, in which he blamed the massacre on Paiute Indians, but even among his own neighbors, there were many rumors of Lee's guilt. Another letter later confessed that he had been involved in the event. Lee was later excommunicated from the church for his involvement.

In 1858 a federal judge came to southwestern Utah to investigate the massacre and Lee's part in it, but Lee went into hiding, and local Mormons refused to cooperate with the investigation. Lee was arrested many years later in 1874 and found guilty. He was executed at Mountain Meadows on March 23, 1877.

THE WALKER WAR

The **Walker War** was another early skirmish in Utah's history. Some local historical accounts claim that the outbreak of the war was because recently baptized **Chief Walkara (Chief Walker)** failed to acquire a Mormon wife. However, it more likely began with a July 1853 confrontation between settlers in Springville and Walkara's tribe members, which resulted in the death of several young tribesmen.

The Walker War primarily consisted of raids conducted against Mormon outposts in central and southern Utah and retaliations by organized pioneers. Walkara left to go to Arizona for the winter, but Wyonah, a member of his band, and other sympathetic Utes continued fighting. During the fall, Utes killed and injured settlers, most of whom were working outside the

CHIEF WALKARA

towns in small groups even though they had been told they needed to stay in large groups. Such attacks occurred in Fillmore, Fountain Green, Santaquin, and Manti. Raids also included the burning of Spring City, which the settlers had already abandoned, and the theft of a large herd of cattle near what is now Spanish Fork.

The Walker War ended through personal negotiations between Brigham Young and Walkara during the winter of 1853 that were finalized in May 1854 in Levan. Although the fighting ended, none of the reasons for the war or the treatment of the natives were resolved. Walkara died in 1855 at Meadow Creek.

THE CIVIL WAR

Utah was also affected by the **Civil War.** Governor Alfred Cumming left Utah quietly on May 17, 1861. Officially, Cumming was on a leave of absence, but the citizens of Utah knew that his quick departure meant that he would not return. Cumming was from the South, and when the war broke out, he returned home to help in the fight, leaving Utah without a governor for a short time.

ABRAHAM LINCOLN

Utah, as a state, did not take part in the war by sending groups of soldiers to fight, although President Abraham Lincoln did request that Brigham Young provide a full company of one hundred men to protect the stagecoach, telegraph lines, and overland mail routes in Green River Country, which they did to assist in the war.

TOPAZ RELOCATION CAMP

Utah also holds a much darker history as the site of the Topaz Relocation Camp. In 1941, America entered World War II. At this time, some individuals in the federal government believed that many Americans of Japanese descent and Japanese-born residents were a threat to the country's security. They felt that these individuals might be traitors to the country. Approximately 120,000 of these individuals living on the West Coast of the United States were forced to leave their homes in California, Oregon, and Washington as a result of Executive Order 9066, signed by **President Franklin Roosevelt.**

Nearly 10,000 left the West Coast area during a "voluntary evacuation" period and avoided internment. Army and National Guard troops soon unjustly removed the remaining 110,000 from their homes. They were eventually moved to various camps around the country, hundreds or even thousands of miles from their homes.

Topaz, one of these internment sites, was located in the state of Utah. A smaller camp also opened for a short time at Dalton Wells, just north of Moab. It was used to isolate a few men considered to be troublemakers before they were sent to Leupp, Arizona.

Topaz was originally called the "Central Utah Relocation Center," but this name was changed when staff realized that the acronym for the camp was C.U.R.C., which was pronounced "curse." The final name of the camp came from Topaz Mountain, which is located in the area.

Topaz was opened September 11, 1942, and

was soon the fifth-largest city in Utah, with over 9,000 internees and staff. It covered an area of nearly 31 square miles, of which only about one square mile was used for housing the internees. It was closed on October 31, 1945.

AERIAL VIEWS OF THE CAMP, THEN AND NOW

THE TWO MEMORIAL PLAQUES AT THE TOPAZ JAPANESE INTERNMENT CAMP

SUFFRAGE

Another source of conflict in Utah revolved around suffrage, or the right to vote, for women.

The first territorial legislature of the Wyoming Territory granted women suffrage in 1869. In the following year, 1870, the Utah Territory did the same, giving women the right to vote in the polls. Because the voting window of Utah came earlier in the year than that of Wyoming, Utah women were the first in the United States to ever cast a vote. What made the situation of Utah so different than that in the rest of the nation was the fact that the Utah women did not push for the right, but it was deemed the right thing to do by nearly all residents of the territory.

As stated earlier in this book, seventeen years later, in 1887, the United States Congress determined that this practice in the Utah Territory was harmful to good

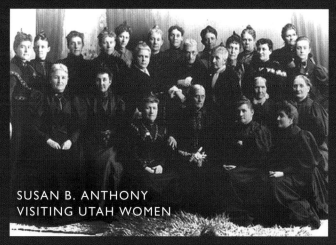

SUSAN B. ANTHONY
VISITING UTAH WOMEN

government and would give complete political control of the territory to the Mormons because nearly all of the voting women were members of the faith. In 1890, Wyoming was admitted to the Union as the first state that allowed women to vote. In 1893, voters of Colorado made that state the second of the women's suffrage states. In 1895, Utah adopted a constitution that restored the right of women to vote, and in 1896, Utah became a state with this right intact.

COLLEGES
AND
UNIVERSITIES

The University of Deseret

Higher education took hold in Utah not long after it was colonized. The first of these schools was the University of Utah. Originally established February 28, 1850, by Brigham Young, it was initially called the **University of Deseret.** The school closed two years later

UNIVERSITY OF DESERET

due to money problems. It reopened in 1867 in the old Council House in what is now downtown Salt Lake City under the direction of David O. Calder, who was a friend of Brigham Young. The school was renamed the **University of Utah** in 1894 and classes were first held on the present campus in 1900.

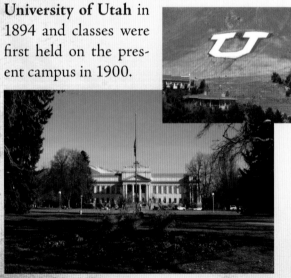

UNIVERSITY OF UTAH

Brigham Young University

October 16, 1875, is commonly held as **Brigham Young University's** founding date. The governing board of the University of

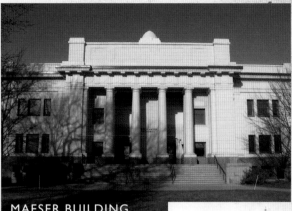

MAESER BUILDING

BRIGHAM YOUNG ACADEMY

Deseret felt an increasing need for a school south of the Salt Lake Valley. They decided to establish the Timpanogos branch of the University of Deseret in Provo. Opened in 1870, it was the only institution of higher learning in Utah County until 1877. The school was then broken off from the University of Deseret and given the name **Brigham Young Academy,** with classes commencing January 3, 1876. Yes, that is correct; BYU and U of U were once part of the same school. In April 1876, Brigham Young's choice for principal arrived, a German immigrant named Karl Maeser. The school later became a University, and in 1903 was named Brigham Young University. Utah now has a tremendous collection of colleges and universities.

THE "Y"

UTAH'S HIDDEN HISTORY

DO YOU KNOW WHERE YOUR FAVORITE COLLEGE OR UNIVERSITY CAME FROM?

YEAR FOUNDED	FORMER SCHOOL NAME	CURRENT SCHOOL NAME	FOUNDED BY
1850	University of Deseret	University of Utah	Utah Territory
1870	Timpanogos University	Brigham Young University	Utah Territory
1875	Salt Lake Collegiate Institute	Westminster College	Presbyterian Church
1886	Part of Latter-day Saint University	LDS Business College	LDS Church
1888	Dixie Academy	Dixie State College	LDS Church
1888	Agricultural College of Utah	Utah State University	Utah Territory
1888	Snow Academy	Snow College	LDS Church
1889	Weber Academy	Weber State University	LDS Church
1897	Branch Normal School	Southern Utah University	State of Utah
1937	College of Eastern Utah	College of Eastern Utah	State of Utah
1941	Central Utah Vocational School	Utah Valley University	State of Utah
1948	Salt Lake Area Vocational School	Salt Lake Community College	State of Utah

CARILLON TOWER

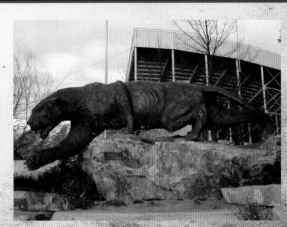

LAVELL EDWARDS STADIUM

2002
WINTER
OLYMPICS

2002 Winter Olympics

2002 Winter Olympics

The year 2002 saw an incredible event that some believed would never happen. Utah hosted the **2002 Winter Olympics.** Salt Lake City was selected as the host city on June 16, 1995. The slogan was "Light the Fire Within." Events were held in Salt Lake City as well as in the mountains at Park City, Ogden, and Provo. The Olympic stadium was Rice-Eccles Stadium at the University of Utah.

The opening ceremonies included country singer LeAnn Rimes singing "Light the Fire Within," the official song of the 2002 Olympics. The Mormon Tabernacle Choir then performed "The Star-Spangled Banner."

The flag found in the rubble at Ground Zero of the World Trade Center Disaster in 2001 was flown, and NYPD officer Daniel Rodriguez sang "God Bless America" and honored those who died in the event.

This Olympics marked the first time an American president opened an Olympic Winter Games held in the United States. **President George W. Bush** was there to do the honors.

In the 2002 games, skeleton returned as a medal sport for the first time since 1948. Also the women's bobsled became an Olympic sport for the first time. Another feature of these games was the emergence of "extreme" sports, such as snowboarding, moguls, and aerials, which had appeared in previous Olympic Winter Games but were very highly watched and publicized in the 2002 games.

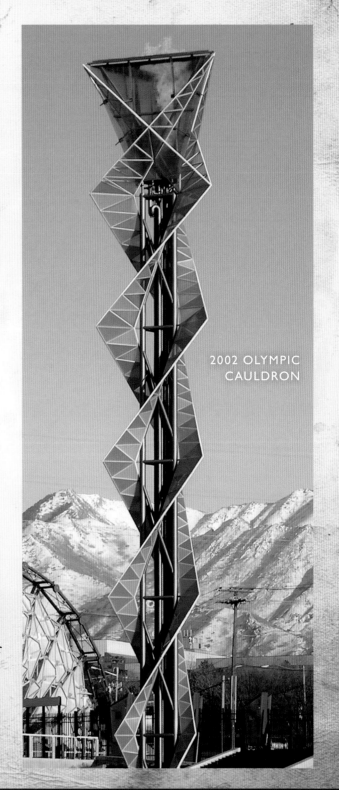

2002 OLYMPIC CAULDRON

2002 OLYMPIC
OPENING
CEREMONIES

2002 OLYMPIC
MEDAL CEREMONY

GOLD AND BRONZE MEDALS

Other memorable moments were American Sarah Hughes winning the gold medal in figure skating and Michelle Kwan receiving the bronze medal. China won its first and second Winter Olympic gold medals, both by women's short-track speed skater Yang Yang. Australian skater Steven Bradbury became the first person from Australia or any other country of the Southern Hemisphere to win a gold medal in the Winter Olympics.

MINING

MINING

Utah has an incredible mining history. It all began in the early 1860s with the arrival of Col. Patrick E. Connor, commander of the Third California Volunteers, who had been sent to Utah in 1862 to keep an eye on the overland mail routes during the Civil War. Connor did not like the Mormons and quickly came up with a plan to remove them from power in the state. Connor believed that if gold, silver, and other precious metals were found in Utah, miners from all over the country would rush into the territory and would overwhelm the Mormons. He sent the men under his command out to prospect, and by doing so he single-handedly opened the precious metals industry in Utah. In 1863 he located gold, silver, and copper deposits, staked claims, and began establishing mining districts.

GOLD

Although states like California and Nevada are noted as high gold producing states, due mainly to the famous gold rushes, Utah produces tens of millions of dollars of gold every year. Since the late 1800s, Utah has produced several billion dollars in **gold** from mines.

GOLD

Gold in Utah can still be found in the Uintah Mountains, the hills of central Utah near Tintic, in Tooele County, near Hanksville, as well as near Park City and in the La Sal Mountains. Rumors and stories tell of many other locations throughout the state where gold has been found, dating back to the time of the Spanish explorers.

SILVER

Over the past century, Utah has also been a high producer of another precious metal, **silver.** Silver does not often get the same attention as gold, but it is still very valuable. Silver was the most important early metal in Utah and remained so until the 1900s. During that

SILVER

time, more than half of Utah's mineral production was silver, which was about 20 percent of the silver produced in the United States. In 1925 Utah mines accounted for 32 percent of the nation's silver. In 1983, the last year for which figures are available, it provided over 10 percent of the silver produced in the United States.

COPPER

Copper is the metal that Utah is most famous for. When the United States entered World War II, copper production brought the **Kennecott/Bingham Canyon Mine—** and Utah—into the national spotlight. In fact, the Bingham Canyon Mine set world records for copper mining and produced nearly

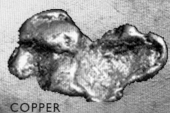

COPPER

MINERS; ELECTRIC MULE CART;
BINGHAM CANYON MINE 1910

BINGHAM CANYON COPPER MINE

30 percent of the copper used by the Allies in bullets and other equipment during World War II.

Mining at the Bingham Canyon Mine has continued since the war, stopping only for a brief period in the 1980s when the copper market dropped. Since that time the mine has continued to produce hundreds of thousands of tons of copper each year, along with large amounts of gold and silver. Today, the Bingham Canyon Mine is the largest open-pit copper mine in the world.

UTAH'S
GEOLOGY

UTAH'S GEOLOGY

In addition to copper, silver, and gold, Utah's **geology** stands out as incredible. The state of Utah is home to a number of **extinct volcanoes.** Many of these were very active millions of years ago and are responsible for lava rock, which is strewn throughout the state. The most recent eruption in Utah history occurred about 600 years ago in the **Black Rock Desert** of Millard County.

STRATOVOLCANOES

Utah was once home to all three types of volcanoes. The **stratovolcanoes** (composite volcanoes) were among the earliest to form. They began erupting as early as 40 million years ago. At this time Utah was much closer to the plate boundaries and the location where the **North American Plate** was being forced over the **Farallon Oceanic Plate.** As a result of the friction of these two plates crossing, along with the Oceanic plate being forced into the mantle, pressurized pools of lava formed and pushed up violently to the surface. Active stratovolcanoes, such as **Mount Saint Helens** in Washington, can still be seen in the western United States.

SHIELD AND CINDER CONE VOLCANOES

Shield and **cinder cone volcanoes** began erupting in Utah nearly 12 million years ago as the earth's crust began to move differently. These volcanoes were the result of pressure from colliding plates being released. When this happened, the land in Utah began to stretch back out, creating holes and cracks in

SANTA CLARA VOLCANO

	THREE TYPES OF UTAH VOLCANOES		
VOLCANO TYPE	**VOLCANO SHAPE**	**TYPE OF ERUPTION**	**EXAMPLES IN UTAH**
Shield Volcano		Quiet—slow lava flows	Cedar Hills Volcano
Cinder Cone		Explosive—cinders	Santa Clara and Snow Canyon Volcanoes
Stratovolcano		Explosive—lava layers and flows	Mt. Belknap and Monroe Peak

the crust where **magma** was able to rise to the surface and form the shield and cinder cone volcanoes.

As you travel throughout the state, you may notice black rock that is often jagged and may even look like it has been melted. This rock was once magma, deep in the earth. It forced its way to the surface and burst out as **lava.** Here on the surface it cooled into rock. This rock takes many shapes, sizes, and forms.

EARTHQUAKES

Utah is also home to earthquakes. Utah has hundreds of **faults** running through it. These can be large, like the famous **Wasatch Fault,** or very small faults that are spread throughout nearly every part of the state. These faults are responsible for the dozens of earthquakes in Utah each year.

Because of Utah's very diverse geological past, all three major classifications of rocks can be found here: **sedimentary, igneous,** and **metamorphic.** Each type of rock can be found in many places throughout the state. Many can even be found right in your own backyard.

SEDIMENTARY ROCK

Sedimentary rock is formed as layers of **sediment,** sand, rocks, mud, clay, and even fossils pile on top of each other. Over millions of years, these individual pieces become stuck to the pieces next to them because of pressure and turn to a solid stone.

Millions of years ago, when Utah was still part of the inland sea, sand was deposited on the ocean bottom as well as the large sand beaches. This sand eventually hardened into sedimentary stone. The solidified sand from this ancient sea can be seen in southern Utah's

Arches National Park. After the stone was formed, the earth began breaking it down again through processes called **weathering** and **erosion.** Wind and water cut away the stone and left incredible formations such as arches and towers. The sandstone that makes up the arches and towering stone columns is what is left of the ancient ocean floor and beaches.

Sedimentary rock filled with fossils can also be found all over the state. Much of the rock found at **Dinosaur National Monument** was created by layers of sand, dirt, and mud covering the bones of ancient dinosaurs. Many times we think of dinosaur bones as the actual bones of the dinosaur or think they have been turned to stone. What actually happened was that the dinosaur's flesh decayed, leaving only the bones behind. These bones were covered

SEDIMENTARY ROCK

DINOSAUR CAST AND FOSSIL

with dirt and over time, as the bones slowly decayed, they were replaced by sediment, leaving casts of the actual bones. A **cast** is sometimes called a mold or replica. These casts are also mixed in with other sediments and create a solid rock, filled with not only stones and sand but also dinosaur bone casts.

IGNEOUS ROCK

Utah is also home to a tremendous amount of igneous rock. Igneous rock begins its life deep within the earth as magma. This rock then travels toward the surface where it either cools underground without ever reaching the surface or bursts through the crust as lava and then cools.

When magma cools slowly underground, you end up with rocks such as **granite,** which is a very hard stone, usually containing quartz crystals of various sizes. Large deposits of granite can be found in the mountains above Salt Lake City. It was these granite (monzonite) deposits that were used to build both the Utah State Capitol building and the Mormon **Salt Lake Temple.**

When magma bursts from the ground and becomes lava, different types of igneous rocks are created, such as **basalt, rhyolite,** and even **obsidian.** These rocks can be found all over the state.

GRANITE

METAMORPHIC ROCK

Metamorphic rock is the third type found in Utah. Metamorphic rock begins its life as either sedimentary or igneous rock. Due to forces within the earth, this rock is then exposed to great pressure and heat. These forces transform the rock into a new rock. Common types of metamorphic rock in Utah include slate, marble, quartzite, and gneiss.

UTAH'S HIDDEN HISTORY

Volcanoes sometimes produce a glass called obsidian. When broken, volcanic glass is sharper than a knife or even a razor blade. Many native peoples in and outside of Utah used obsidian to make arrowheads, spearheads, and other tools because of its natural sharpness.

OBSIDIAN ARROWHEADS

TIMPANOGOS CAVE

These various rock types have created some of the most incredible sites in our state. **Timpanogos Cave National Monument** is just one such place. Over millions of years, water has seeped through cracks in the ground, slowly dissolving the rock. This creates holes in the earth better known as caves. As water continues to move, the caves continue to grow.

The water also begins bringing new material into the caves and starts the process of filling them in again with new sediment. This is exactly what happened inside Timpanogos Cave. The soft limestone dissolved long ago and left a large network of caverns. Then the water above the caves continued to dissolve and carry tiny amounts of limestone with it. This began to seep back into cracks in the cave. As it dripped in, it deposited tiny bits of limestone on top of other bits and created what appear to be large stone icicles known as **stalactites.** The same thing happened as water hit the floor of the cave and caused similar stone points to grow upward. These are called **stalagmites.**

At times the stalactites and stalagmites grow together and form large columns. These columns can eventually form new walls and fill in parts of the cave. The Wasatch Fault has been a major factor in the formation of Timpanogos Cave. The fault has created cracks and splits in the ground, providing a perfect path for the water to follow as it soaks through the ground.

Timpanogos Cave is also known for its many **helictites** that grow throughout the cave. Helictites are formed as water seeps into the

cave and creates a hollow straw. When the water stops flowing due to drought or other causes, the end of the tube closes up. When water starts flowing again it looks for a new opening and either adds to the old straw or creates a new one that might even be connected to the old one. These tubes can grow hanging down like stalactites, or they can grow sideways and even up from time to time. After millions of years, this action creates what looks like starfish, coral, or even long, thin fingers.

The truth is that most of Utah's National Parks and Monuments are here as a result of millions of years of rocks, water, and wind working with and against each other to build up and tear down the earth's crust. Utah has had this happen much more than nearly any other location on earth, and that is why people come from all over the world to view the results.

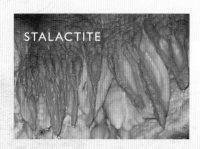
STALACTITE

HELICTITES

STALACTITE

THE HEART OF TIMPANOGOS

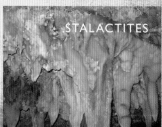
STALACTITES

UTAH'S
NATIONAL
TREASURES

Utah has 5 National Parks, 6 National Monuments, 1 National Recreation Area, and 1 National Historic Site. This is far more than any other state and nearly as many as most other states combined.

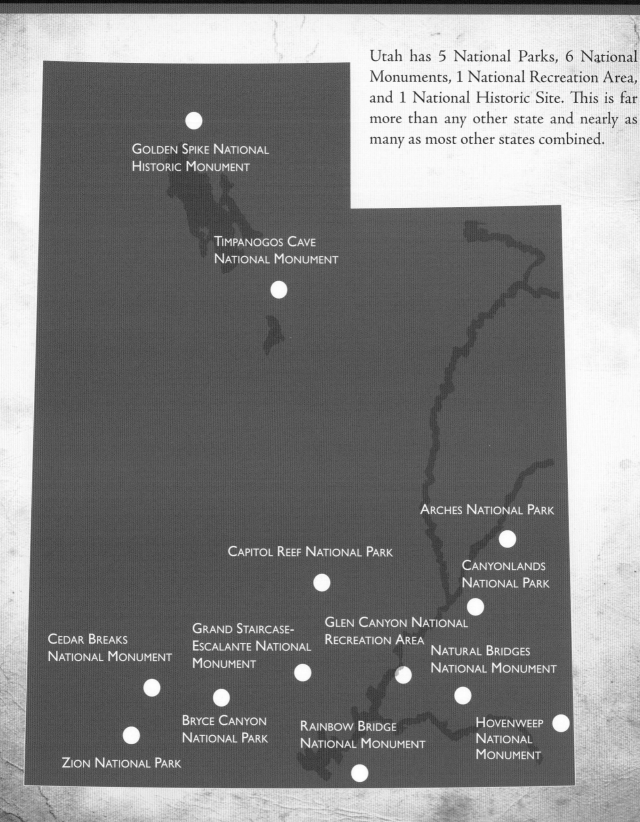

GOLDEN SPIKE NATIONAL HISTORIC MONUMENT

TIMPANOGOS CAVE NATIONAL MONUMENT

ARCHES NATIONAL PARK

CAPITOL REEF NATIONAL PARK

CANYONLANDS NATIONAL PARK

GLEN CANYON NATIONAL RECREATION AREA

CEDAR BREAKS NATIONAL MONUMENT

GRAND STAIRCASE-ESCALANTE NATIONAL MONUMENT

NATURAL BRIDGES NATIONAL MONUMENT

BRYCE CANYON NATIONAL PARK

RAINBOW BRIDGE NATIONAL MONUMENT

HOVENWEEP NATIONAL MONUMENT

ZION NATIONAL PARK

DELICATE ARCH

Arches National Park

Arches National Park is located in the southeast part of the state. Arches is 119 square miles in area. The park includes the famous **Delicate Arch.**

Arches form over time as water seeps into cracks, joints, and folds in the rocks. Ice then forms in the holes and cracks, expanding and putting pressure on surrounding rock, causing pieces to break off. Wind and water later clean out the loose and broken rock. When this happens, often a structure called a **fin** remains. Wind and water again attack these fins until, in some cases, chunks of rock tumble out. Many damaged fins collapse, while others survive with missing center sections. These become arches.

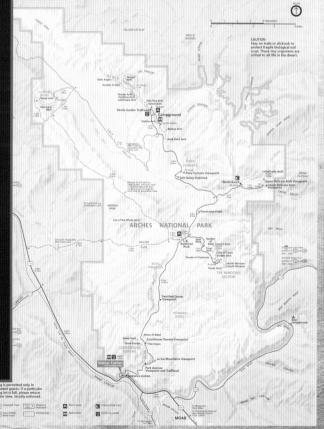

BRYCE CANYON HOODOOS

BRYCE CANYON NATIONAL PARK

Bryce Canyon National Park is located in the southwest part of the state. Bryce Canyon is 56 square miles in area. The park is most famous for its unique structures called **hoodoos,** and like Arches National Park, it too has a variety of stone arches.

Hoodoos are stone pillars that rise into the air in unique shapes. They are created by water and wind washing away stone. The softer stone is eroded and weathered first, leaving the harder stone remaining. These stone hoodoos come in a tremendous variety of colors ranging from red and orange to white and brown.

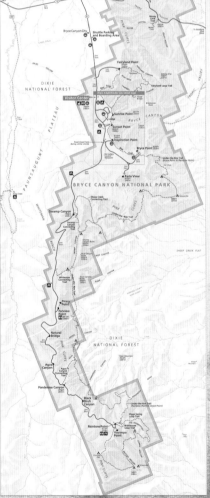

CANYONLANDS NATIONAL PARK

Canyonlands National Park is located in the southeast part of the state. Canyonlands is 527 square miles in area. It is famous for its many canyons carved into the earth by rivers and streams running through the area.

The formations in Canyonlands were created primarily by water eroding the soil and rock. Most of the rock in the park is sandstone, formed by ancient seas long ago. As flowing water ran over it, small particles broke off and washed away. After millions of years, deep canyons formed where huge amounts of rock have been completely eroded away.

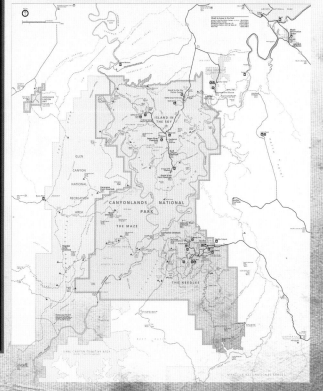

NAVAJO SANDSTONE DOMES

CAPITOL REEF NATIONAL PARK

Capitol Reef National Park is located in the south-central part of the state. Capitol Reef is 378 square miles in area. It is famous for its large domes formed from Navajo sandstone.

Capitol Reef was formed millions of years ago when continental plates collided and folded the earth's crust in an "S" shape. As the soil and rock over this fold eroded, a series of large white sandstone domes formed. Many people thought these domes looked like the dome on the United States Capitol building. When it became a national park, the idea stuck, and it was called Capitol Reef.

CEDAR BREAKS NATIONAL MONUMENT

Cedar Breaks National Monument is located in the southwest part of the state. Cedar Breaks is nearly 5 square miles in area. It is often referred to as a smaller version of Bryce Canyon National Park. The monument is filled with hoodoos and other incredible rock formations.

GRAND STAIRCASE-ESCALANTE NATIONAL MONUMENT

The Grand Staircase-Escalante National Monument is located in the south-central part of the state. The Grand Staircase is nearly 2,968 square miles in area. This is the youngest of Utah's National treasures and was created in 1996 by **President Bill Clinton.**

The Monument was controversial from the start. The creation ceremony was held at Grand Canyon National Park in Arizona, and not in the state of Utah. The Utah legislators and governor were only notified 24 hours in advance. This was seen by many as a way to gain votes for President Clinton in the state of Arizona.

On the other hand, the monument is very beautiful. It is named for the layered rock that forms a staircase-looking structure. The park is also home to arches, hoodoos, and even some very well preserved dinosaur fossils.

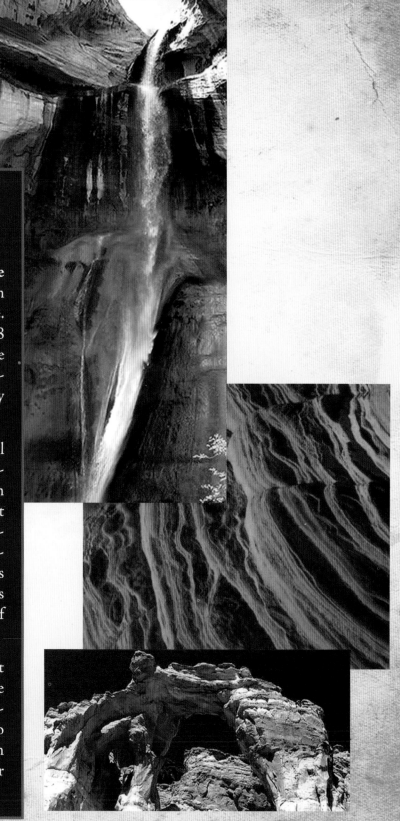

LAKE POWELL

GLEN CANYON NATIONAL RECREATION AREA

Glen Canyon National Recreation Area is located in the southeast part of the state. The Glen Canyon Area is nearly 1,959 square miles. The area's main attraction is Lake Powell, which is the second largest man-made reservoir in the United States. The recreation area also contains artifacts, carvings, and dwellings of many early native Utah cultures such as the Anasazi (Ancestral Puebloans).

GOLDEN SPIKE NATIONAL HISTORIC SITE

The Golden Spike National Historic Site is located in the northwest part of the state. The site is 4 square miles in area. This is the site of the historic joining of the Transcontinental Railroad in 1869. A spike made of gold was driven into the railroad in celebration of this meeting. This was the first real transportation route connecting the eastern United States to the West. Visitors to the site can see a replica of the Golden Spike and replica trains from the time period.

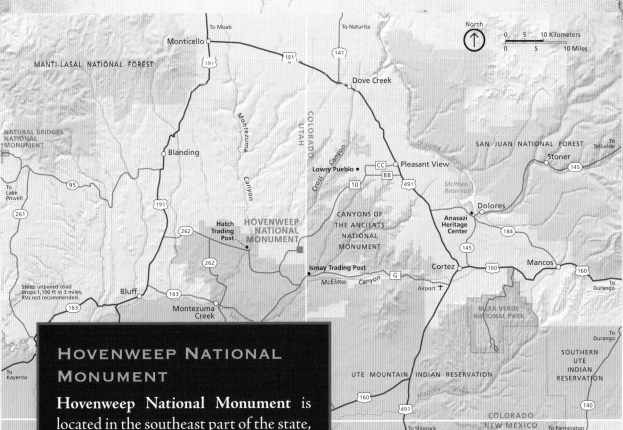

SQUARE TOWER

HOVENWEEP NATIONAL MONUMENT

Hovenweep National Monument is located in the southeast part of the state, spilling over into Colorado. The monument is just over 1 square mile in area. The monument contains the ruins of the ancient Anasazi (Ancestral Puebloan) culture.

The ruins are the remains of large stone buildings, pieced together like modern bricks. It is thought that some of these buildings were built around AD 1200. The most popular on the Utah side of the park is called Square Tower. It is a large square-shaped tower that rises high into the air. Hovenweep is a great tribute to what was accomplished by our ancient native peoples.

OWACHOMO BRIDGE

NATURAL BRIDGES NATIONAL MONUMENT

Natural Bridges National Monument is located in the southeast part of the state. Natural Bridges is nearly 12 square miles in area. It is famous for its three very large archlike structures called bridges.

It was Utah's first national monument. President Theodore Roosevelt created the monument in 1908. Natural Bridges holds the second and third largest natural bridges in the world. The three bridges, called Kachina, Owachomo, and Sipapu, were all given Hopi names. There is also evidence of at least two other collapsed bridges in the park. In addition to the bridges, visitors can see Horsecollar Ruin, one of the most well preserved ancient Anasazi (Ancestral Puebloan) ruins ever discovered.

RAINBOW BRIDGE NATIONAL MONUMENT

Rainbow Bridge National Monument is located in the southeast part of the state. The monument is only ¼ square mile in area. Resting on the shores of Lake Powell, you will find the very large natural bridge. It was formed of red sandstone during the late Triassic and early Jurassic periods. The bridge still serves as a sacred location for many of our native peoples, so please be sure to show proper respect when visiting the monument.

TIMPANOGOS CAVE NATIONAL MONUMENT

Timpanogos Cave National Monument is located in the north-central part of the state. The monument is nearly ½ square mile in area. The cave is located in American Fork Canyon in the Wasatch Mountains. Timpanogos Cave is best known for its stalactites, stalagmites, and helictites.

The monument is one of the most popular in the state, attracting over one million visitors each year. Because the cave is still growing and changing due to water, it is important that visitors do not touch the walls or any other stone formations in the cave. Touching them leaves oils from your skin, which makes the rock too slick for other minerals to stick to.

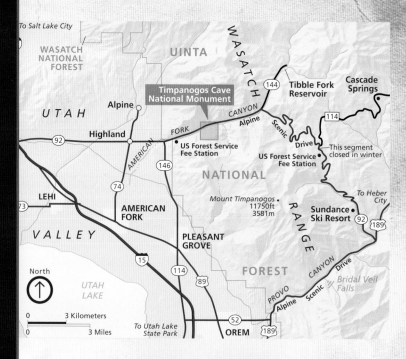

ZION NATIONAL PARK

Zion National Park is located in the southwest part of the state. The park is 229 square miles in area. Zion is known for its towering rock mountains and its deep canyons. It was designated a national park by President Taft and named Mukuntuweap National Monument in 1909, but the name was later changed to Zion National Monument in 1918. It became a national park in 1919.

The word *zion* is an ancient Hebrew word meaning place of refuge or sanctuary. The park has served as a sanctuary for nearly 300 of the state's bird species, 75 mammal species, and 32 reptile species. It also served as a home for many of our native peoples such as the Anasazi (Ancestral Puebloans), Fremont, and Paiute.

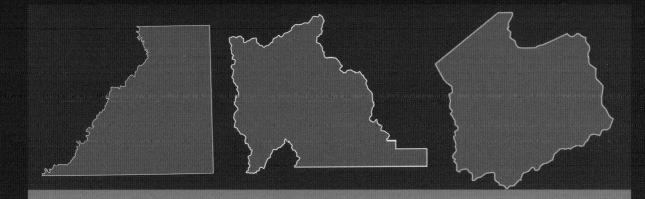

UTAH'S
COUNTIES

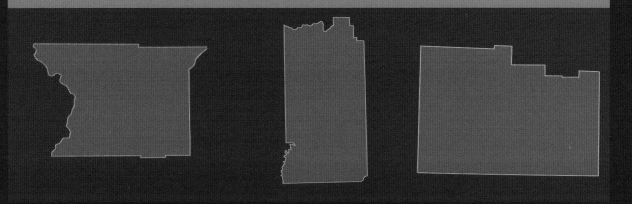

Utah's 29 Counties also make the state a destination for millions of people each year. Each county has its own history and features that make it unique. Each county also works together to keep Utah functioning as a state. We will look briefly at each one in alphabetical order.

BEAVER COUNTY is located in the southwestern part of the state. Its county seat is Beaver City. Beaver County is 2,586 square miles in area. Its highest point is Delano Peak, which reaches 12,173 feet above sea level. Beaver County is the home of Butch Cassidy. Fathers Escalante and Domínguez, Jedediah Smith, and John C. Frémont also visited this area. The county gets its name from the many beaver once found there. Beaver has also produced gold, silver, and copper for many years.

BOX ELDER COUNTY is located in the northwestern part of the state. The county seat is Brigham City. Box Elder County is 5,614 square miles in area. Its highest point is Bull Mountain, which stands 9,920 feet above sea level. Box Elder County is the home of the golden spike. This was the final spike joining the Transcontinental Railroad together. Many caves, such as Danger Cave and Hogup Cave, are located in the county and contain the remains of many native tribes.

CACHE COUNTY is located in the northern part of the state. The county seat is Logan City. Cache County is 1,171 square miles in area. Its highest point is Naomi Peak, which is 9,979 feet above sea level. Cache County was home to the Shoshone culture. Early trappers and traders such as Jim Bridger explored it extensively. Cache County can claim to be the home and final resting place of Old Ephraim. Utah State University is also located in the county.

CARBON COUNTY is located in the eastern part of the state. The county seat is Price City. Carbon County is 1,476 square miles in area. Its highest point is Monument Peak at 10,452 feet above sea level. Carbon County was inhabited by the early Fremont culture. The county got its name from the abundant coal resources there. The main element in coal is carbon. Carbon County is also home to the College of Eastern Utah, which holds a replica of the Huntington Mammoth.

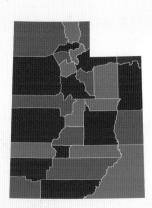

DAGGETT COUNTY is located in the northeastern part of the state. The county seat is the Town of Manila. Daggett County is 682 square miles in area. Its highest point is Eccentric Peak, which towers 12,276 feet above sea level. Daggett County was the last of the state's 29 counties to be organized. It is home to Flaming Gorge Reservoir, which generates power for much of the western United States. Daggett is also home to the Uintah Mountains, which is the only major mountain range in the United States that runs east to west.

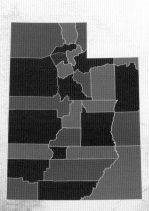

DAVIS COUNTY is located in the north-central part of the state. The county seat is Farmington City. Davis County is the smallest county, being only 268 square miles in area. Its highest point is Thurston Peak, which rises 9,706 feet above sea level. Davis County is the home of Hill Air Force Base. The county is also home to Antelope Island. The island is located in the Great Salt Lake and is the home of about 600 bison.

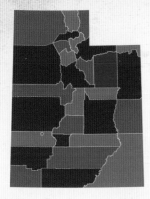

DUCHESNE COUNTY is located in the northeastern part of the state. The county seat is the Duchesne (do-Shane) City. Duchesne is 3,255 square miles in area. Its highest point is Kings Peak, which is the highest point in Utah, soaring 13,528 feet above sea level. Duchesne also holds four of the five highest points in Utah, making it the highest county in the state. Duchesne County was colonized in a different manner than most of Utah. Settlers here obtained 160-acre parcels under the federal Homestead Act. These homesteaders were required to prove that they intended to farm the land. After five years of living there, making improvements, and paying $1.25 per acre, homesteaders were given a title to their land. Today Duchesne is still home to farmers and ranchers, but it also has several oil fields.

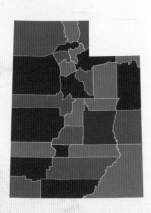

EMERY COUNTY is located in the eastern part of the state. The county seat is Castle Dale City. Emery is 4,439 square miles in area. Its highest point is East Mountain at 10,743 feet above sea level. Emery County is the true home of the Huntington Mammoth. No other mammoth has ever been found at such a high elevation. The county has also played a huge part in the creation of energy and is home to coal deposits and power plants. The Spanish Trail passes through the county, and the county was also home to the Fremont and Ute Tribes.

GARFIELD COUNTY is located in the south-central part of the state. The county seat is Panguitch City. Garfield is 5,158 square miles in area. Its highest point is Mount Ellen, which is 11,522 feet above sea level. Garfield County is the home of Bryce Canyon National Park. It has been home to the Fremont, Anasazi (Ancestral Puebloan), Paiute, and Ute tribes. The county was named after President James A. Garfield, the twentieth president of the United States, who was assassinated in 1881.

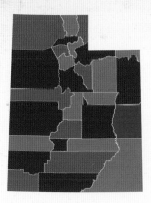

GRAND COUNTY is located in the eastern part of the state. The county seat is the City of Moab. Grand is 3,689 square miles in area. Its highest point is Mount Waas, which stretches 12,391 feet above sea level. Grand County is home to Arches National Park. The county was home to the early Anasazi (Ancestral Puebloan) culture, as well as more recent tribes. Grand County has existed as a farming and livestock area but has also seen mining of various metals and uranium. The county was named for the Grand River, which was later renamed the Colorado River.

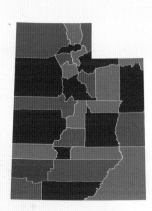

IRON COUNTY is located in the southwestern part of the state. The county seat is the Town of Parowan. Iron is 3,300 square miles in area. Its highest point is Brian Head Peak, which stands 11,307 feet above sea level. Iron County was also home to the ancient Anasazi (Ancestral Puebloan) culture. It held part of the Spanish Trail and was passed through by Fathers Escalante and Domínguez. The Paiute tribe also inhabited the county. Iron County is also the home of Southern Utah University.

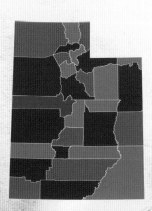

JUAB COUNTY is located in the central part of the state. The county seat is Nephi City. Juab is 3,412 square miles in area. Its highest point is Ibapah Peak, which extends 12,087 feet above sea level. Juab County has had its share of famous visitors over the centuries. Fathers Escalante and Domínguez, Jedediah Smith, and John C. Frémont have all found their way through the area. The Goshute Reservation is located in the northwest corner of the county. Mining has also played a big part in the county's history. Gold, silver, copper, lead, and zinc have all been found and mined there.

KANE COUNTY is located in the south-central part of the state. The county seat is Kanab City. Kane is 3,904 square miles in area. Its highest point is Andy Nelson Peak at 10,027 feet above sea level. Kane County is the proud home of Lake Powell, named after John W. Powell, who explored the area decades before. Both the ancient Anasazi (Ancestral Puebloan) and the more modern Paiute tribe made their homes in the county. Kane County can also be considered Utah's movie star. It has been the set for nearly 100 movies, including *Stagecoach*, *The Greatest Story Ever Told*, *The Outlaw Josey Wales*, and both the 1968 and 2001 *Planet of the Apes* movies. It also served as the setting for a number of TV series including the *Lone Ranger*, *Gunsmoke*, and *Grizzly Adams*.

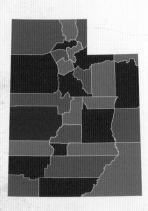

MILLARD COUNTY is located in the western part of the state. The county seat is Fillmore City. Millard is 6,818 square miles in area. Its highest point is Mine Camp Peak at 10,222 feet above sea level. Millard County contains the record of Utah's oldest residents. Over the years, thousands of trilobites have been found there. Millard County is also the home of the town of Fillmore, which was Utah's State Capital for a time and still holds the original statehouse. The Topaz Relocation Camp remains are also located in the county; they stand as a record of this nation's struggle for true freedom. Millard and its county seat get their name from our thirteenth president, Millard Fillmore.

MORGAN COUNTY is located in the northern part of the state. The county seat is Morgan City. Morgan is 603 square miles in area. Its highest point is Thurston Peak, which stands 9,706 feet above sea level. Morgan County was used by both the Shoshone and Ute Tribes for a long period of time. Today Morgan has more privately owned land than any other county in Utah. This land is used mainly for farming and raising animals. Morgan has another secret it keeps—it provided many of the railroad ties used in building the Transcontinental Railroad because of the lumber industry it had at the time.

PIUTE COUNTY is located in the south-central part of the state. The county seat is the Town of Junction. Piute is 754 square miles in area. Its highest point is Delano Peak, which rises 12,173 feet above sea level. Piute County is named for the Piute tribe of Utah. The county is also home to Big Rock Candy Mountain. The mountain is a volcanic formation that consists of rock that is yellow, red, orange, and white, closely resembling candy colors. It got its name when the song "Big Rock Candy Mountain" was released in 1928 and, as a joke, some local residents placed a sign near it identifying it as the Candy Mountain. The name stuck, and the mountain is still called that today. Gold, silver, lead, and zinc were mined successfully in this county for many years.

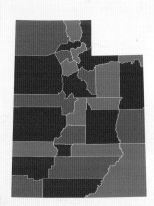

RICH COUNTY is located in the northern part of the state. The county seat is the Town of Randolph. Rich is 1,034 square miles in area. Its highest point is Bridger Peak, which is 9,255 feet above sea level. Rich County can be considered the coldest county in the state. The town of Woodruff holds the state record for the coldest temperature ever recorded. On February 6, 1899, the temperature reached a bitter minus fifty degrees Fahrenheit (-50°F). This is 86 degrees below freezing. Rich County is home to Bear Lake, which is one of Utah's largest lakes and is popular with campers, boaters, and water-skiers.

SALT LAKE COUNTY is located in the northern part of the state. The county seat is Salt Lake City. Salt Lake is 764 square miles in area. Its highest point is Twin Peaks at 11,489 feet above sea level. Salt Lake County, of course, holds Utah's State Capitol. Atop a hill on the north end of Salt Lake City stands the grand State Capitol Building. This county has played a major part in every law and regulation to happen in the state. Salt Lake City is also home to the University of Utah (former University of Deseret), which houses the 2002 Winter Olympic Stadium. The county is also home to many professional sports teams, such as the Utah Jazz.

SAN JUAN COUNTY is located in the southeastern corner of the state. The county seat is the City of Monticello. San Juan is the largest county in size, coming in at 7,725 square miles in area. Its highest point is Mount Peale, which stands 12,721 feet above sea level. San Juan County is one of the nation's most visited tourist destinations. It is home to Canyonlands National Park, Natural Bridges National Monument, Rainbow Bridge National Monument, Hovenweep National Monument, and the Glen Canyon National Recreation Area. San Juan was home to the ancient Anasazi (Ancestral Puebloan) and to the past and present-day Navajo peoples. Gold miners also worked the area early on, but it was uranium that made many rich. Today, oil and gas are being pumped in a few areas of the county.

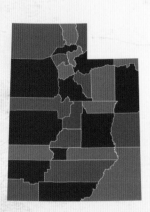

SANPETE COUNTY is located in the central part of the state. The county seat is Manti City. Sanpete is 1,597 square miles in area. Its highest point is South Tent, which towers at 11,285 feet above sea level. Sanpete County is a rural area. Its unchanged beauty since the 1800s has attracted people from all over the world. Spring City is one such place. The town has a very large number of old buildings that have been restored. It has so many that the entire town has been designated a National Historic District. The town was also home to Hiram Bebee. The Fairview Museum holds a replica of the Huntington Mammoth that was found in the mountains above Fairview. Sanpete County is also the home of Snow College.

SEVIER COUNTY is located in the central part of the state. The county seat is Richfield City. Sevier is 1,976 square miles in area. Its highest point is Mount Marvine at 11,610 feet above sea level. Sevier County is covered by forests. In fact, nearly half the county is composed of national forest lands. The county is also home to Fremont State Park, one of the best preserved dwelling sites of the ancient Fremont Indians. Part of the Old Spanish Trail crosses through the county. In recent times, oil and natural gas resources have been found in the county.

SUMMIT COUNTY is located in the northeastern part of the state. The county seat is Coalville City. Summit is 1,849 square miles in area. Its highest point is Gilbert Peak, which towers 13,442 feet above sea level. Summit County is perhaps the ski capital of the state. The county hosted most of the 2002 Olympic Games skiing events. Park City is still home to Utah's Olympic Park. The county has also been home to a major part of Utah's historic mining industry, providing metals such as gold, silver, lead, and zinc.

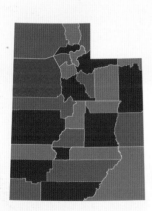

TOOELE COUNTY is located in the northwestern part of the state. The county seat is Tooele (toowil'a) City. Tooele is 6,923 square miles in area. Its highest point is Deseret Peak, which is 11,031 feet above sea level. Tooele County could be considered the fastest place on earth. Located in the county, near the Great Salt Lake, is the Bonneville Speedway. This is a track built on salt where some of the fastest vehicles in the world race. Many world records have been broken here over the years in various types of vehicles. The salt from the lake is also harvested and sold for use in foods. There is a good chance that the salt in your house may come from right here in Tooele.

UINTAH COUNTY is located in the northeastern part of the state. The county seat is Vernal City. Uintah is 4,487 square miles in area. Its highest point is Eccentric Peak, which rises 12,276 feet above sea level. Uintah County is home to part of Dinosaur National Monument. Its rich fossil deposits draw visitors from all over the world. The county is also rich in other ways. Large deposits of oil have been found there, and wells pump the oil from the ground so it can be used throughout the country.

UTAH COUNTY is located in the central part of the state. The county seat is Provo City. Utah is 2,014 square miles in area. Its highest point is Mount Nebo, at 11,928 feet above sea level. Utah County was discovered by Fathers Escalante and Domínguez as part of their expedition in the 1770s. The county was the original home of the Ute tribe before they were forced out by settlers. Utah County is home to the famous Timpanogos Cave National Monument, and Brigham Young University and Utah Valley University also call Utah County their home.

WASATCH COUNTY is located in the north-central part of the state. The county seat is Heber City. Wasatch is 1,191 square miles in area. Its highest point is Mount Cardwell, which stands 10,743 feet above sea level. Wasatch County is primarily a rural area. Much of the county is used for farming, while a large portion is used for fishing, boating, camping, golfing, and other outdoor activities. This area also has heated springs that bubble up from the ground. Very high temperatures, deep within the earth, heat underground water and force it to the surface, where it is used for many purposes.

WASHINGTON COUNTY is located in the southwest corner of the state. The county seat is the City of St. George. Washington is 2,422 square miles in area. Its highest point is Signal Peak, at 10,365 feet above sea level. Washington County is a real hot spot, boasting the highest average temperatures in all of Utah. Things were hot here millions of years ago too, as volcanoes forced lava throughout the area. Washington was also home to groups of Anasazi (Ancestral Puebloans), whose dwellings can still be seen throughout the area. Washington County holds many points of interest, including Zion National Park, Dixie State College, and one of Brigham Young's former homes.

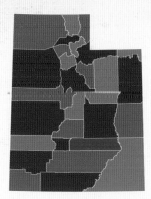

WAYNE COUNTY is located in the south-central part of the state. The county seat is the Town of Loa. Wayne is 2,486 square miles in area. Its highest point is Bluebell Knoll, which sits 11,328 feet above sea level. Wayne County is the home of Canyonlands National Park as well as Capitol Reef. Mainly used for farming and ranching, Wayne county has always been a great place to be an animal. Some of Utah's most interesting fossils of the Ice Age come from the area, including the camel, ground sloth, horse, and bison.

WEBER COUNTY is located in the northern part of the state. The county seat is Ogden City. Weber is 644 square miles in area. Its highest point is Willard Peak, which stands 9,764 feet above sea level. Weber County has had an interesting history. It was first mapped by John C. Frémont after his visit in 1848. Weber County was also home to John M. Browning, the famous gun maker. Weber State University is located there.

INDEX

225-65 Million BC	Mesozoic Era (Age of Dinosaurs)
225–193 Million BC	Triassic period
193–136 Million BC	Jurassic period (First dinosaurs in Utah)
136–65 Million BC	Cretaceous period
1776	Fathers Francisco Atanasio Domínguez and Silvestre Vélez de Escalante depart from Mexico on an exploratory journey north.
July 29, 1776	Domínguez and Escalante leave Santa Fe with 12 Spanish men and 2 Ute boys.
September 12, 1776	Domínguez and Escalante cross what later becomes the Utah border near what is now Dinosaur National Monument.
January 2, 1777	Domínguez and Escalante return to Santa Fe after a journey of 1,700 miles.
1824	James (Jim) Bridger enters Utah with a group of trappers and traders.
1830	The Book of Mormon is published after translation is complete.
April 6, 1830	Joseph Smith organizes The Church of Jesus Christ of Latter-day Saints (then called the Church of Christ).
1837	The Latter-day Saint bank in Kirtland fails due to the national economy.
1838 to 1839	Mormons are driven from Missouri after Governor Lilburn W. Boggs issues the "Extermination Order," stating that the Mormons must leave the state or be killed.
1840 to 1849	John C. Frémont travels the trail from Santa Fe to Los Angeles, and names it the Spanish trail.
1843	John C. Frémont leads an expedition to Utah. He names the Spanish Fork River in honor of Fathers Domínguez and Escalante.
1844	Joseph Smith becomes a candidate for president of the United States
June 27, 1844	Joseph Smith and his brother Hyrum are killed in Carthage, Illinois.
1847	Jim Bridger meets the Mormon settlers headed west and provides them with hand-drawn maps.
July 24, 1847	Brigham Young enters the Salt Lake Valley.
1848	The pioneers are saved by flocks of California gulls which ate the black crickets that attacked the settlers' crops.
1848	Weber County is first mapped by John C. Frémont.
1849	Brigham Young and the settlers create the State of Deseret and petition for statehood.
1849	Brigham Young sends families to Tooele Valley to colonize.
1850	The federal government creates the Utah territory.
February 5, 1850	The University of Utah is established by Brigham Young (then called The University of Deseret)
1851 to 1856	Fillmore, Utah, serves as the Utah territorial capital.

1851	Brigham Young sends families to Box Elder, Pahvant, Juab, and Parowan Valleys to colonize.
February 3, 1851	Brigham Young becomes the first governor of the Utah Territory.
1852	The University of Deseret (University of Utah) closes due to money issues.
1853	The Mormons purchase Fort Bridger from Jim Bridger for $8,000.
July 1853	A confrontation between settlers in Springville and Chief Walkara's tribe leads to the death of several tribesmen.
Fall 1853	Utes kill and injure settlers in what is later known as the Walker War. Attacks occur in Fillmore, Fountain Green, Santaquin, and Manti.
Winter 1853	Negotiations take place between Chief Walkara and Brigham Young.
May 1954	Negotiations are finalized and the Walker War comes to an end.
1855	Chief Walkara dies at Meadow Creek.
January 1855	John Browning is born in Ogden, Utah.
1856	John C. Frémont runs for president.
1856	Brigham Young sends families to Cache Valley to colonize.
1857	President Buchanan removes Brigham Young as governor of the Utah territory and sends a 2,500-man military force to put in Alfred Cumming as governor.

1857	Fort Bridger is destroyed by the Mormons to impede the march of Albert Sidney Johnston's army.
July 1, 1857	Martha Maria Hughes (Cannon) is born near Llandudno, Wales.
September 11, 1857	Mormon militiaman led by John D. Lee, with possible help from Paiute allies, kill 120 settlers in Mountain Meadows.
1858	A federal judge comes to investigate the Mountain Meadows Massacre and John D. Lee's involvement.
June 26, 1858	Johnston's army arrives in Salt Lake City and finds it abandoned. Cumming becomes governor and makes peace with the Mormons.
May 17, 1861	Governor Alfred Cumming leaves office to help the Confederate army in the Civil War.
1862	Morrill Anti-Bigamy Act is passed in the U.S. Senate. The act was never implemented.
1862	Patrick E. Connor is sent to Utah to watch the overland mail routes during the Civil War.
1863	Construction begins on the transcontinental railroad.
1863	Patrick E. Conner locates gold, silver, and copper deposits in Utah. He stakes claims and establishes mining districts.
April 9, 1865	The Black Hawk Indian War commences. Around 70 settlers are killed in the war.

April 13, 1866	Robert LeRoy Parker (Butch Cassidy) is born.
1867	John Wesley Powell begins exploring the Rocky Mountains and the Green and Colorado Rivers.
1867	The University of Deseret (University of Utah) reopens under the direction of David O. Calder
Fall of 1867	Chief Black Hawk makes peace with the Mormon settlers.
1868	A peace treaty is signed and the Black Hawk Indian War is officially over, but some raiding and killing continues until 1872.
1869	John Wesley Powell takes his most famous journey. He and his party travel 900 miles down the Green River in Wyoming, through Utah, and into the Grand Canyon.
May 8, 1869	The Union Pacific Railroad Company meets the Central Pacific Railroad Company, completing the transcontinental railroad at Promontory Summit.
May 10, 1869	The golden spike is driven into the tracks to celebrate the completion of the transcontinental railroad.
1870	Utah Territory grants women suffrage, and Utah women become the first in the United States to vote.
1870	The Timpanogos branch of The University of Deseret opens in Utah County.
September 26, 1870	Chief Black Hawk dies of tuberculosis.
1874	John D. Lee is found guilty of killing 120 settlers in the Mountain Meadows Massacre.
October 16, 1875	Brigham Young University is founded (then called Brigham Young Academy).
January 3, 1876	Classes commence at Brigham Young Academy (Brigham Young University).
April 1876	Karl Maeser arrives to serve as principal of Brigham Young Academy (Brigham Young University).
1877	Brigham Young Academy breaks off from the University of Deseret.
March 23, 1877	John D. Lee is executed for his involvement in the Mountain Meadows Massacre.
1881	U.S. President James A. Garfield is assassinated. Garfield County is later named after him.
January 12, 1886	Edmunds-Tucker Bill is passed by the U.S. Senate. All property of the LDS church worth more than $50,000 must be given to the federal government.
1887	The federal government deems suffrage for women in Utah harmful as it would give complete political control to the Mormons.
1894	The University of Deseret is renamed The University of Utah.
March 4, 1895	Utah leaders meet in the new Salt Lake City and County Building and write the new constitution for Utah.
May 8, 1895	The new Utah constitution is signed.

November 5, 1895	The new constitution is ratified, and state officials and legislators are elected. A petition is again sent to the federal government for Utah to be made a state.
January 4, 1896	President Cleveland declares Utah a state. Women in Utah keep their suffrage.
November 3, 1896	Martha Maria Hughes Cannon becomes the first woman to be elected as a U.S. senator.
February 6, 1899	Rich County records the coldest temperature in Utah history, -50 degrees Fahrenheit.
1900	Classes at the University of Utah commence on the present campus.
1903	Brigham Young Academy is renamed Brigham Young University.
April 19, 1906	Philo T. Farnsworth is born in Beaver, Utah.
1908	President Theodore Roosevelt creates the Natural Bridges National Monument, Utah's first national monument.
November 3, 1908	A delivery man is robbed near San Vicente, Bolivia, by two Americans (possibly Butch Cassidy and the Sundance Kid).
1909	Utah State Legislature passes three bills to help build a new capitol building.
1909	The Mukuntuweap National Monument is named.
1911	The Sego Lily is made Utah's state flower.
1912	Construction begins on the new Utah State Capitol building.
1914	Gavrilo Princip uses a Browning handgun to assassinate Archduke Franz Ferdinand, beginning World War I.
1916	Construction on the Utah State Capitol building is finished.
1918	The Mukuntuweap National Monument is renamed Zion National Monument.
1919	Zion National Monument becomes a national park.
August 2, 1923	Frank Clark kills "Old Ephraim" the grizzly bear.
1925	An alleged family reunion is held by Butch Cassidy and his family, according to his sister.
1925	Utah mines account for 32 percent of the nation's silver.
1926	Philo T. Farnsworth forms a partnership with George Everson to develop his television ideas.
1928	Philo T. Farnsworth holds a demonstration of his new television system for the press.
1928	The song "Big Rock Candy Mountain" is released, and Big Rock Candy Mountain in Piute County is soon named after the song.
1929	The television system is improved, and the first live human images are transmitted by Philo T. Farnsworth.

1941	America enters World War II, and Japanese residents are forced to leave their homes as a result of Executive Order 9066, signed by President Franklin D. Roosevelt.
1942	Philip Johnston convinces Major General Clayton B. Vogel that Navajo can be used as code in World War II.
May 1942	First Navajo code talker recruits enter boot camp.
September 11, 1942	Topaz Relocation Camp opens.
October 31, 1945	Topaz Relocation Camp closes.
1955	California gull becomes Utah's state bird.
1945	Hiram Bebee (possibly the Sundance Kid) is sentenced to death after killing a marshal.
1968	Original Planet of the Apes film is released (filmed largely in Kane County).
1974	Edwin Jacob Garn is elected to the Senate.
1980	Senator Garn is re-elected to the Senate in a landslide election, receiving 70 percent of the vote.
1983	Utah mines account for 10 percent of the nation's silver.
April 12, 1985	Space Shuttle Discovery launches from Florida. Utah Senator Edwin Jacob Garn is aboard.
April 19, 1985	Space Shuttle Discovery completes its mission.

1994	Utah State legislature passes a bill making copper the state mineral.
June 6, 1995	Salt Lake City is selected as the host city for the 2002 Winter Olympics.
1996	President Bill Clinton establishes The Grand Staircase-Escalante National Monument.
1997	The Bonneville Cutthroat replaces the Rainbow Trout as Utah's state fish.
2001	Remake of Planet of the Apes is released (filmed largely in Kane county as was the original).
2002	Winter Olympics held in Salt Lake City and surrounding areas.

ACKNOWLEDGMENTS

THANK YOU to my parents Val and Sherie Sorensen for instilling a true love of the great state of Utah in me and for dragging their children all over the state every chance they got.

THANK YOU also to my wife, Rachelle, and daughters Alexis, Adriana, and Aryiah for allowing me to pursue my dreams and providing me with support and encouragement.

SPECIAL THANK YOUS for pictures, text, and information to:

The Utah Geological Survey

The Utah State Historical society

Dr. Kenneth Carpenter

College of Eastern Utah

Utah State University

Brock Sisson

The Utah State Governor's Office

THANK YOU also to Cedar Fort, Inc., for their belief in this project and especially to Angela Olsen, Heidi Doxey, Katreina Eden, and Trevor Redd. Thank you for all your hard work.